SHOPPING BAG DESIGN

THE BEST OF SHOPPING BAG DESIGN

Judi Radice

Jackie Comerford

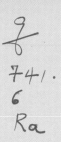
Distributor to the book trade in the United States:
Rizzoli International Publications, Inc.
597 Fifth Avenue
New York, NY 10017

Distributor to the art trade in the United States:
Letraset USA
40 Eisenhower Drive
Paramus, NJ 07653

Distributor in Canada:
Letraset Canada Limited
555 Alden Road
Markham, Ontario L3R 3L5, Canada

Distributed throughout the rest of the world by:
Hearst Books International
105 Madison Avenue
New York, NY 10016

Library of Congress Cataloging-in-Publication Data

Radice, Judi.
  Shopping bag design.

  1. Shopping bags. 2. Graphic arts. I. Title.
NK8643.3.R33 1987   741.6   87-61167
ISBN 0-86636-053-0

Book Design: Daniel Kouw

Color separation, printing, and binding by
Toppan Printing Co. (H.K.) Ltd. Hong Kong
Typesetting by McFarland Graphics, Inc.

STAFF

Publisher	**Herb Taylor**
Project Director	**Cora Sibal Taylor**
Executive Editor	**Virginia Christensen**
Editor	**Wanda P. Jankowski**
Art Director	**Richard Liu**
Production Manager	**Kevin Clark**
Artist	**Donna O'Hare-Patterson**

Dedication

In gratitude for the years of encouragement, support and patience, we dedicate this book to our families.

Acknowledgements

Countless designers, retailers and distributors have provided us with the information and insights we needed to write this book. First, we wish to thank those individuals who agreed to be interviewed and quoted. In particular, though, we wish to thank a few individuals whose efforts would otherwise remain unsung.

Nathan Gluck of A.I.G.A. provided us with an historical context. Carol Chamberlin and her former students from the San Francisco Academy of Art gave us a vision of the future. Bobbi Rosenthal and Meredith Lewin were our presence in New York when we couldn't be there. Thanks, too, to John Hicks for being there when we needed him most. Kathryn Hetzner's endless dedicated hours on the telephone provided much of the research for the book. Deborah Case, David Magennis and our seemingly tireless typist, Chip Krug, supplied critical commentary and needed perspective when inspiration flagged. Bernard Stalder was kind enough to donate both paper and the use of his office equipment during the critical early stages of the book. Michael Rawls provided us with several valuable leads.

Finally, all the manufacturing companies we contacted were tremendously helpful in supplying leads, obtaining releases and guiding us through the maze of bag manufacturing. In particular, we are grateful to E. Marvin Jacobson of Champion International for critical commentary and assistance in compiling the glossary.

Thanks are also due to the designers, retailers and artists whose visions made reality provided the impetus for the book in the first place. Without all of you, this book would not be possible. Many Thanks.

Contents

Introduction

The creative explosion in
shopping bag design which has
characterized the past 15 to 20
years is in direct response to
the rampant consumerism in
current American culture. To a
much greater extent than any
other graphic art application,
shopping bags are an accurate
reflection of the concerns of
present-day society.

Designer shopping bags are a
relatively recent phenomenon.

Prior to the early 1970's, they were almost unknown. Two-income families and higher economic expectations on the part of the average consumer have created a climate suitable for specialized, artistic bags.

In this book, we will explore the conditions which have nurtured the development of the designer bag, discuss techniques for meeting current design challenges, and provide a tantalizing glimpse of possible future developments in the genre.

Like any other endeavor in commercial art, the effectiveness of shopping bag design is dependent upon a clear understanding of visual,

marketing and technical considerations.

This book will provide the reader with a grounding in current manufacturing techniques that permit the development and realization of a workable design. Each of the manufacturing processes has its own set of advantages and limitations. The key to a successful design is understanding these and planning the design accordingly. What works for one printing method may need adjustment to accommodate another method.

The purpose of this book is to explore the development of shopping bag design, examine current trends, and illuminate possible strategies for the future. We have thoroughly enjoyed writing it and hope that you will find it a valuable tool in future design projects.

Judi Radice
Jackie Comerford
San Francisco, California

Build a Better Bag

What is a Shopping Bag?

Initially, the answer to this question might seem obvious. But if the objective is to design and "build" a better shopping bag, it is useful to begin with a precise definition.

A shopping bag is a three-dimensional object equipped with two handles. It is usually constructed of paper or plastic and has two major functions: to carry a variety of small objects conveniently and to advertise the establishment which provides it. Small shopping bags, such as those used for cosmetics, are designed to carry one purchase. The larger size is designed to transport a number of smaller packages.

Four major groups usually participate in the development and production of a shopping bag: graphic designers; retailers or other purveyors of goods; distributors; and manufacturers. A number of other individuals, such as copywriters, architects and marketing research specialists, may also be involved. This chapter will explore the interaction among these groups as well as provide insights into the considerations unique to the perspective of each of them.

Design Specifications

The original purpose of shopping bags was to carry a variety of small objects from one place to another—conveniently and safely. Transport is still the primary function; aesthetics and advertising remain secondary, though they have become increasingly important in the 1970's and 1980's.

The materials used in a shopping bag must be strong, comfortable for a person to carry, and accept inks and dyes readily. Most shopping bags are still made of paper or paper strengthened with plastic ("synthetic paper"). Over the past decade, however, plastic has made inroads into paper's dominance of the market.

The comfort of a shopper carrying a bag is one of the most important design considerations. The most beautiful graphic will remain unseen if nobody wants to carry the bag. The handles should be easy on the carrier's hand. Nothing should protrude from the bag to snag on clothing. The material used to make the bag should have a pleasant texture. The bag should be a convenient size to carry. Too long a bag will force the shopper to carry his or her arm at an unnatural angle. Market research, including reference to the standard height and weight charts produced by the insurance industry, provides the designer with information on customer preferences and comfort specifications so that these factors may be taken into consideration during the design process.

Shopping bags can be made in a wide variety of sizes and shapes. The most familiar is a hollow oblong with two stiffened cord handles. There are also dress packs, small paper, cloth and plastic bags for cosmetics, hat boxes, garment bags and bags which can be substituted for gift wrapping. Cost considerations prevent most stores from using more than a few of the many sizes and shapes available. Technical considerations—how a two-dimensional graphic becomes a three-dimensional bag—dictate some design criteria.

Designs that Work

When designing a graphic for use on a shopping bag, the artist must visualize the environment in which it will appear. Unlike a print ad, signage or even a menu, the shopping bag is a three-dimensional, moving medium. This factor can be a design strength, if the concepts of animation are incorporated into the design. For example, wrapping a design entirely around the bag can be a very eye-catching technique. Designs work differently in motion than on a flat surface. The visual background against which the design will appear is beyond the artist's control. The milieu of the shopping bag is the shifting pageant of a city street.

Only very strong materials can be used in the creation of a shopping bag. Yet sturdy Kraft paper, synthetic paper and plastic do not accept inks and dyes in the same way as fine printing paper. Textures are somewhat limited as well, although this area is broadening as new production techniques are developed.

Obviously, the size of the bag and the distance at which it will be viewed dictate the size of the graphics. Very small type and intricate patterns may be difficult to see and, consequently, lose their effectiveness when the shopping bag is in normal use and seen from a distance. Strong color contrasts work sometimes, even in the context of a small pattern.

Finally, the way in which shopping bags are made places several restrictions on design. The seam in the gusset and the gluing required there make matching a pattern in this area complicated due to variations in registration. But the gussets can also conceal design surprises, relevant copy and credit information about the bags themselves, provided the designer is aware of the production considerations and can accommodate them.

Manufacturing Solutions

Three basic types of printing are used in the production of shopping bags: offset gravure, offset lithography, and flexography.

Offset gravure is the oldest printing technique. It involves etching the images with acid into flexible metal plates. Because of high initial costs, gravure is extremely impractical for images which will change frequently. On the other hand, it offers the cleanest, most consistent reproduction.

Offset lithography involves transfer of an image from one cylinder to another; the second cylinder, in turn, transfers the image to the paper.

Flexography involves the use of rubber or, more recently, photopolymer plates. The easiest way to visualize these plates is as a kind of giant rubber stamp. Recent advances have led to process flexography—a significant improvement in the basic technique. Process printing involves tiny dots of color; flexography, the application of solid color. Process flexography is a marriage of the two techniques. At the moment, they might best be described as "newlyweds," but the technique is rapidly improving.

The vast majority of shopping bags are produced via flexography. One of flexography's drawbacks is that the art is four generations from the original when it is printed; this can result in shrinkage of as much as two percent. If the designer is aware of this factor at the conceptual stage and incorporates the information, production of the bag will be easier for all concerned.

In general, flexography is the most practical printing technique from an economic standpoint for most projects. Only when very large quantities are involved does offset printing, which affords the designer more flexibility, become practical.

Finishing Touches

A shopping bag's effectiveness and relative beauty is dependent upon far more than the illustration and graphic design. Use of matte or glossy inks, high-gloss laminate, electron beam or ultraviolet coatings, and selection of the proper material and style for the handle all affect the appearance of the finished product.

Handle types can range from twisted paper or twine inserted on a production line to hand-applied, flat-braid fabric cord. Choice of one type over another should be governed as much by the point of view behind the design as by economics. Finish and handle type should be keyed to enhance and complement the design.

Although they are attractive and "glamorous," high-gloss finishes are not appropriate for every shopping bag design. The needs—and surroundings—of the establishment for which the bag is produced should be considered when choosing a finish or a bag material. Noisy materials would be inappropriate for a theatre or musical performance environment. Brown Kraft paper might not work as well as mylar or plastic to reflect the image of a chic boutique. Climatic conditions and the nature of the objects to be carried are also factors to be considered when choosing the material for the body of the bag. Plastics are a popular choice in changeable or rainy climates; paper is easier to set at one's feet on a crowded bus.

Successful shopping bags are created when a wide variety of individuals incorporate their various areas of expertise into a united effort to produce a unique design—an extension of the store's architecture, a response to a local trend, a practical and aesthetically pleasing or exciting solution to a specific problem. The following chapters examine some of these successful solutions.

COPY RE: SERVICING GREAT
RESTAURANTS THROUGHOUT THE
YEARS & THEIR CONSENT TO
PROVIDE RECIPES.

2 RECIPES

1½ lb. ROUND LOAF

FULL COLOR AS PER
LOGO COLOR SPEC.

SAY PO-DEEN

BOUDIN.

Shopping Bag Title:	**Boudin Bakeries**
Establishment:	**San Francisco French Bread Company, Oakland, CA**
Designer/Art Director:	**Primo Angeli**
Firm:	**Primo Angeli Inc., San Francisco, CA**
Manufacturer:	**Champion International, Walden, NY**
Distributor:	**Zellerbach Paper, San Francisco, CA**
Materials	
Paper:	**White Kraft**
Handle Type:	**Flat Paper**

The place this bag is seen by many is at the airport—it leaves town on various planes hundreds of times every day. The design, part of the Smithsonian Museum's permanent collection, works well for several reasons. It portrays bread's simplicity and wholesomeness in a vaguely 19th century design. The copy was developed to reinforce the message of the uniqueness of the bread. Finally, though the design was planned for lithographic printing, it was produced via flexography. The design worked even though the two techniques are very different. Because bread is relatively heavy, the handles are reinforced with thread for extra strength.

Shopping Bag Title:	**Lane Bryant Shopping Bag**
Establishment:	**Lane Bryant, New York, NY**
Art Director:	**Robert P. Gersin**
Firm:	**Robert P. Gersin Associates, New York, NY**
Manufacturer:	**Equitable Bag Company, Long Island City, NY**
Materials	
Paper:	**Kraft**
Handle Type:	**Ivory Plastic**

The staggered lozenges in four colors are more than an eye-catching design. They are part of a coordinated program involving in-store signage and point of purchase collaterals. The design reflects the range of sizes available. Since Lane Bryant's customers are "special size" women, it was critical that the message be conveyed subtly and with dignity. The lozenges are an elegant design solution.

Shopping Bag Title:	**Tradewell Grocery Bag**
Establishment:	**Tradewell Group, Renton, WA**
Designer:	**Jack Anderson/ Mary Hermes/ Cheri Huber**
Art Director:	**Jack Anderson**
Firm:	**Hornall Anderson Design Works, Seattle, WA**
Illustrator:	**Jani Drewfs**
Distributor:	**Food Services of America, Kent, WA**
Manufacturer:	**Princeton Packaging Inc., Tacoma, WA**
Materials	
Paper:	**Kraft**

Special stamps were developed to promote various departments within the store. These, used in conjunction with the copy, create an interesting pattern on the bags. The copy itself was carefully crafted to support the images of high-quality, broad selection and personal service the store wished to project. An extension of this basic design is used for direct mail advertising, in-store flyers, signage and advertising.

Bag Title:	**Prototype**
Designer/Art Director:	**Seymour Chwast**
Firm:	**Pushpin Studios,**
	New York, NY
Illustrator:	**Seymour Chwast**

Shopping bags and boxes are three-dimensional objects. To take full advantage of the fact that all sides will eventually be seen, the designer has used an animation effect to draw the viewer's eye to additional sides beyond the one first glimpsed. The procession of bicycles is endless, with the front wheel of one becoming the back wheel of the next. This concept makes the shape and use of the shopping bag a design strength, rather than a problem to be resolved.

Shopping Bag Title:	**West End Marketplace**
Establishment:	**West End Marketplace, Dallas, TX**
Designer:	**Paul Black**
Art Director:	**Paul Black/Don Sibley**
Firm:	**Sibley/Peteet Design, Dallas, TX**
Illustrator:	**Paul Black**
Materials	
Paper:	**Clay Coat**
Handle Type:	**Twisted Paper**

This bag was designed as a grand-opening giveaway for a complex of retail and restaurant establishments. Balloons, confetti and the building itself supported the grand opening theme. Because the bag was designed for a one-time use, printing costs had to be limited. The solution was to use offset printed labels on generic solid color bags. For small establishments wishing to achieve distinction, this is an elegant and cost-effective approach.

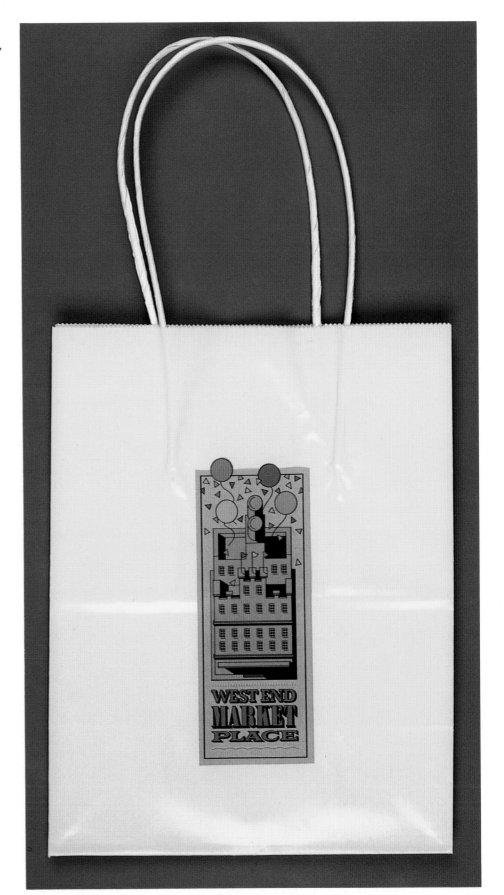

Shopping Bag Title:	**Coty Awards/** **Coty Botanicals**
Establishment:	**Coty International,** **New York, NY**
Designer:	**Dominick Sarica**
Firm:	**One and One Design** **Consultants Inc.,** **New York, NY**
Photographer:	**Roy Volkmann—side with** **woman's face** **Colin Cooke—side with** **cosmetic products**
Distributor:	**Modern Arts Packaging** **New York, NY**
Materials	
Paper:	**Coated**
Coating:	**Laminate**
Handle Type:	**Soft Cord**

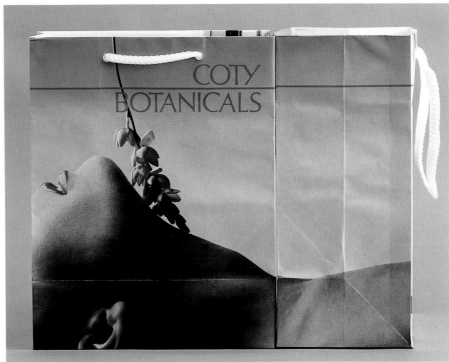

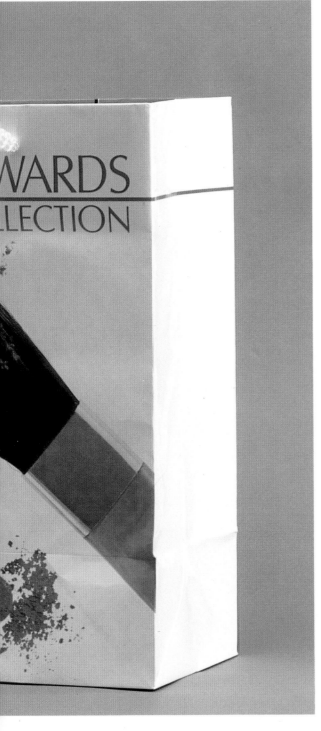

Cosmetic promotion bags are probably the most demanding to design and produce. While cosmetic sales are built on the unspoken promise of wish fulfillment, image integrity demands that color matches be exact and the images perfectly registered. The model's skin is subtly contrasted with a delicate spray of flowers on one side. Vivid swirls and sprays of products in the colors offered adorn the other. The design suggests what is possible, without being specific as to how to achieve it—essential to the marketing of this type of product.

Shopping Bag Title: **"5 Senses of Christmas"**
Establishment: **I. Magnin,**
San Francisco, CA
Designer: **Brian Collentine**
Art Director: **Art Shipman/I. Magnin**
Firm: **Brian Collentine Design**
Illustrator: **Brian Collentine**
Manufacturer: **Equitable Bag Company,**
Long Island City, NY

Materials
Paper: **Clay Coat**
Handle Type: **Twisted Paper**

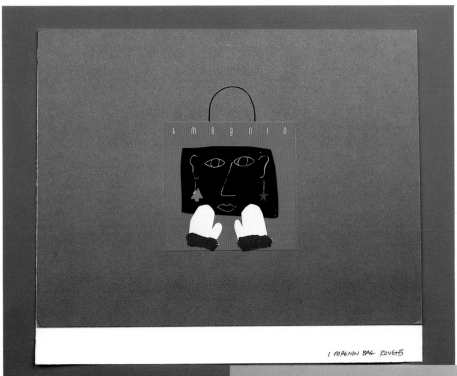

The composite sketches for these I. Magnin bags were developed, for the most part, with cut-outs of construction paper and ink. The use of layers of paper cut-outs gives the images a needed component—the third dimension of depth—that is so characteristic of all shopping bag designs. In some instances, textured paper has been incorporated into the original design. Note that, even in these prototypes, the designer has remained true to the idea of simplicity. A bold, simple image works much better on a shopping bag than a complex one.

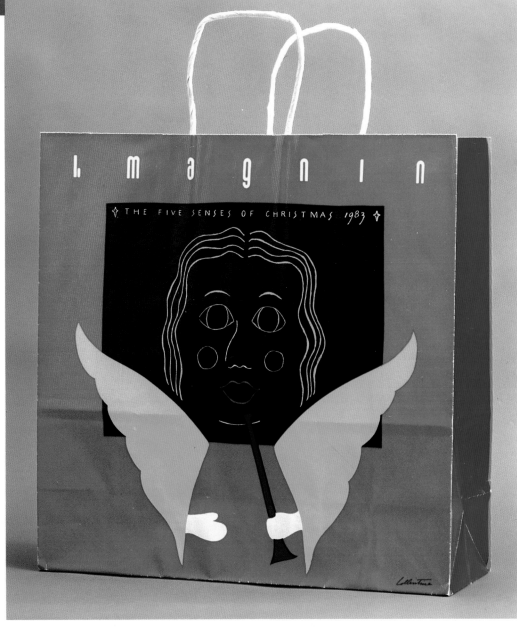

Shopping Bag Title: **Boutique Bazaar**
Establishment: **Boutique Bazaar, Hong Kong**
Designer: **Alvin Chan**
Art Director: **Alan Chan**
Firm: **Alan Chan Design Company, Wanchai, Hong Kong**
Materials
Paper: **Coated**
Handle Type: **Fabric**

The panther was selected as a design motif to convey the idea that the boutique's clothing is elegant, energetic and dynamic. The wraparound illustration lends a sense of movement to the design and suggests interesting uses for the bag in in-store displays.

Shopping Bag Title:	**Alan Flusser (menswear)**
Establishment:	**Alan Flusser Men's Salon,** New York, NY
Designer:	**Tana Klugherz**
Art Director:	**Tana Klugherz**
Firm:	**Tana & Company,** New York, NY
Printer of Labels:	**Conceptual Litho,** New York, NY
Distributor:	**Modern Arts Packaging,** New York, NY
Materials	
Paper:	**Leatherette**
Handle Type:	**Maroon Plastic**
Special Finishing:	**Embossed Stickers**

This men's store, located in a penthouse on East 52nd Street in New York City, needed a clubby, 1930's feeling for its bag. The design solution involved custom labels and a leatherette paper to achieve a quality and style reminiscent of the past. The label design is also used on stationery, business cards and forms, and sewn-in labels to maintain a consistent image.

Shopping Bag Title:	**Christmas Bags**
Establishment:	**Bergdorf Goodman,** New York, NY
Designer/Art Director:	**Dain Marcus**
Firm:	**Dain Marcus,** New York, NY
Illustrator:	**Dain Marcus**
Manufacturer:	**S. Posner & Sons,** New York, NY
Materials	
Paper:	**Kraft**
Coating:	**Matte Finish, Varnished**
Handle Type:	**Twisted Paper**
Special Finishing:	**Metallic Inks**

The design challenge here was to develop a concept which would work both for Christmas and for a promotion on India. The design had to be elegant, and reflect the personality of the store, but also be inexpensive to produce. In light of this latter consideration, flexography was the printing method selected.

Shopping Bag Title: **Bermuda**
Establishment: **Bermuda Department of Tourism, New York, NY**
Agency: **Foote Cone & Belding**
Manufacturer: **PAK 2000, Mirror Lake, NH**
Materials
Bag: **Metallized Low Density Polyethylene**
Handle Type: **Soft Cord**
Special Finishing: **Flexographic**

Used as a promotional piece at conventions and by travel agencies, this sturdy polyethylene bag depicts the island of Bermuda in gold metal stamping. Both the bag's sturdiness and the comfortable, long handle make the bag an attractive choice for carrying literature. The attention the designer has paid to the end-user's needs helps make the design work.

◀ Shopping Bag Title: **J. Riggings Poly Bag**
Establishment: **J. Riggings, Atlanta Speciality Retailing, Norcross, GA**
Designer: **Scott Bolestridge**
Art Director: **Robert P. Gersin**
Firm: **Robert P. Gersin Associates, New York, NY**
Manufacturer: **Plastic Packaging Corp., Kansas City, KS**
Distributor: **Piedmont National, Atlanta, GA**
Materials
Bag: **Plastic**
Handle Type: **Die Cut**

This bag was developed to harmonize with a new design for a men's clothing store. The background photos are details based on two photo murals in the store. Use of a coarse dot screen makes the images incomprehensible at close range. Only when viewed at a distance do the pictures of casual and tailored clothing become clear. Since a shopping bag is usually viewed from a distance on a street, this is a very effective visual technique.

Interviews

Marvin Auerbach
Manager, Print Production
GERMAINE MONTEIL
Cosmetic Company

Robert Gersin
Principal
ROBERT P. GERSIN ASSOCIATES
Industrial Design/Marketing

Nancye Green
Partner
DONOVAN & GREEN
Designer/Marketing

Alex Lindsay
Principal
MODERN ARTS PACKAGING BY DESIGN
Distributor/Design

Bill Weiss
Principal
WEISS & SONS
Distributor
Glendale, NY

John Jay
Vice President, Creative Director
BLOOMINGDALE'S
Retailer/Designer

Seymour Chwast
Director
PUSHPIN STUDIOS
Illustrator/Designer

CHAPTER 2

Shopping bags are the most pervasive form of graphic art. For the general public, shopping bags are, unlike posters or the carefully-designed menus of elegant restaurants, an element of daily life. From the secretary who transports lunch in a small plastic shopping bag to the college student who totes laundry to the nearest laundromat, shopping bags are a useful adjunct to daily life.

In this chapter, the shopping bag is examined from the point of view of the professionals who create them. Presented are interviews with the staff of retail establishments, manufacturers, graphic design studios and companies which specialize in the creation of a cohesive corporate and merchandising identity.

Marvin Auerbach
Manager, Print Purchasing
Germanine Monteil, **New York, NY**

"Every designer should check with the manufacturer and review the art before going too far into the design process. You can eliminate a lot of potential production problems in the early stages of design."

Marvin Auerbach has spent most of his adult life producing shopping bags. He had a front-row seat for the tremendous upsurge in creativity experienced by the industry over the past 15 to 20 years. "There were no changes for many years—everything was conventional brown or white Kraft paper, with simple handles." Auerbach has no one explanation for the sudden interest in more imaginative design but notes that, "the technique was always there."

Once people became interested in doing more creatively designed bags, the trend snowballed. "After the creative era came into the picture, you found you could do more and more with shopping bags. The manufacturers themselves became more creative with the existing technology."

This creative spurt eventually slowed, owing partly to the manufacturers' caution in investing heavily in new industrial plants. Theirs, after all, is the heaviest outlay for equipment. "Sheet run bags are the most flexible for innovative designs but the finishing techniques are tricky. These *could* be handled by machinery. In practice, they are finished by hand, sometimes outside the United States."

Mr. Auerbach's years in the industry have given him an intuitive understanding of the process by which a graphic and marketing idea becomes a finished shopping bag. This is especially important in the cosmetics industry, where coordinated packaging is the norm.

Since he works in the cosmetic industry, Auerbach requires exact color matches and very fine registration. Flesh tones and actual models' faces are visuals which cannot be "fudged." Germaine Monteil often uses its bags only for in-store display. The shorter runs involved permit them to use a more technically exact (albeit more expensive) process that would not be feasible in large quantities.

"I know, from experience, how much a bag will cost to produce. I use a distributor to help me find the best method to produce it at the best price.

Shopping Bag Title:	**Small Red Bag**	This bag was designed to carry small samples. Solid red was chosen to give the bag importance and to present a colorful display at the counter. The soft cord handles make the customer feel special walking away with the gift.
Establishment:	**Germaine Monteil Cosmetics Corporation, New York, NY**	
Designer/Art Director:	**Berett Fisher**	
Firm:	**Germaine Monteil, New York, NY**	
Distributor:	**Modern Arts Packaging, New York, NY**	
Materials		
Paper:	**Clay Coat**	
Coating:	**Film Laminate**	
Handle Type:	**Soft Loop One Knot**	

Distributors buy in volume and have a lot of clout with the manufacturers. They can get results for us that we wouldn't get as quickly on our own."

To Auerbach, the key to producing a good shopping bag is planning. "Most people forget one thing when they're designing bags. When you put them together, you may have as much as a quarter of an inch variance—it's the nature of the machinery. . . . It's virtually impossible to match a continuous design, particularly through the gussets." His point is that the designer can avoid production problems—and cost over-runs—simply by reviewing the proposed design with the manufacturer at an early stage in the development process.

If the design and execution become a two-step, coordinated process, the success of the project is assured. "It's like the tip of an iceberg . . . The more you get into it, the more variations you see. You're not limited to shapes and designs . . . you can do almost anything."

Robert P. Gersin
Robert P. Gersin Associates, **New York, NY**

"Shopping bags are walking billboards that are going
to be seen by other potential customers."

Robert Gersin heads a design company which
specializes in the creation of a cohesive image,
whether for a corporation or an institution. As
someone who deals in what he calls the "visual
vocabulary" of color and form, he understands the
importance of a well-designed shopping bag to a
retail establishment's success.

"We design three-dimensionally . . . We get as
real as we can as quickly as we can . . ." he says. In
Gersin's view, the packaging, whether a shopping
bag or a gift box, should set the final seal of
approval on a customer's purchase. What he seeks
in shopping bag design is "post-purchase
satisfaction." The customer should feel that, by
the very fact of his having come home with such
a beautiful and/or stimulating shopping bag, the
purchase must have been a good one. The
importance of this marketing concept cannot, in
Gersin's opinion, be overstressed.

Packaging must also follow the function for
which it is designed. For example, Gersin once
designed a line of shopping bags for a series of
Italian food items created by Marcella Hazan for
Bloomingdale's. Because he was dealing with pasta
and its attendant sauces, Gersin understood the
packaging must be not only attractive, but also
sturdy. Accordingly, he selected plastic, rather than
paper, as the medium for the carrier.

At its best, says Gersin, a shopping bag is "like
getting a present . . . it reinforces the desire to go
back to the same store."

Shopping Bag Title:	**Build Your Wardrobe At . . .**	Designed as a prototype for use primarily in store windows, the bag's theme and execution support a revamped interior design and a new retailing concept. The "build your wardrobe" theme is underlined by the closet doors and hautboy-style dresser. The door with the oval inset is reminiscent of an armoire—also know as a wardrobe—a subtle visual pun.
Establishment:	**Casual Corner, Enfield, CT**	
Designer:	**Scott Bolestridge**	
Art Director:	**Robert P. Gersin**	
Firm:	**Robert P. Gersin Associates, New York, NY**	
Manufacturer:	**Prototype only—limited use for display.**	
Materials		
Paper:	**Kraft**	
Handle Type:	**Plastic**	

Gersin specializes in total identity programs so he has the luxury of designing a shopping bag or auxilliary packaging to coordinate with the overall product environment. This means he has ample time to design the shopping bag in conjunction with the "overall image-building program."

Gersin understands and uses the wide variety of tools available in graphic design to "whet the appetite" of the consumer. "Variety and texture" and "color as a means of visual communication" are an important part of the image-building he accomplishes for a wide variety of clients.

Unfortunately, according to Gersin, "the retailer is often unaware of the image building potential or the rewards from producing a bag, nor do they often exercise much concern beyond the cost." The designer must educate the retailer in the many advantages of using a colorful, provocative bag. "Don't worry about how much the first sale costs you in terms of the packaging. It's worth spending a reasonable percentage of product cost on packaging because of the reinforcement . . . you work to build a second sale or a third."

Shopping Bag Title:	Marcella Hazan's Italian Kitchen
Establishment:	Bloomingdale's "The Main Course," New York, NY
Designer:	Candis Cain
Art Director:	Robert P. Gersin
Firm:	Robert P. Gersin Associates, New York, NY
Illustrator:	Candis Cain
Distributor:	Valprod, New York, NY
Manufacturer:	Amko Plastics, Cincinnati, OH
Materials	
Bag:	Plastic
Handle Type:	Die Cut

In marketing frozen convenience foods, plastic is far more practical packaging than paper. As an added bonus, the tomato red, wheat and soft brown are more vivid than they would be on paper. The program is witty and sophisticated, yet emphasizes the "homemade goodness" of the food products.

Nancye Green
Donovan & Green,
New York, NY

"The shopping bag is the tip of the iceberg . . . the essence of image . . . the haiku."

Nancye Green holds degrees in Urban Studies and Environmental Design. Her partner, Michael Donovan, studied veterinary medicine before pursuing a course at Parsons School of Design. With such multi-faceted backgrounds of the principals, it is not surprising that Donovan & Green as a firm has achieved such an eclectic mix of successful projects.

Green's approach to shopping bag design is clearly influenced by her experience in designing interiors and exhibits. "The graphics on a shopping bag, for a retail establishment—or any kind of public space—are an extension of the place." Green's training permits her to see the shopping bag as a three-dimensional, *moving* object . . . a kind of mobile extension of in-store architecture. The effectiveness of this unusual point of view is amply demonstrated by her work with Barneys New York.

Barneys New York, traditionally a men's store, first opened a 'women's penthouse' in the mid-1970's, then a full-sized women's store. "The shopping bag for the women's store was one of the most important considerations."

Donovan & Green developed the signature shopping bag at the same time the interiors were being designed. "The same attention to detail that went into the store design had to go into the shopping bag. The Pressman family, owners of the store, were interested in getting every single detail exactly right—and devoted the time to achieve it. The shopping bag goes out on the street and represents the store."

The design solution for the Barneys New York shopping bags involved extensive research. The men's store bags are the color and texture of the leather of club chairs in discreet men's clubs. The women's bags are also in leather-texture. The high quality paper used for these is not merely imprinted in black but *made* black during the manufacture of the paper; the finished bags are stamped in silver.

Before designing the women's bags, Donovan & Green conducted the extensive research alluded to above. "A lot of attention was given to the sizes and shapes of the bags. Women's heights were considered. The *comfort* of carrying the bag was an important consideration." One of the unusual design details which resulted from this research was the decision to use shoulder straps, rather than the more commonly used double carrying handles. Barneys New York shopping bags are durable, chic and easy to use. "Besides the look

of it, how it feels to carry it is important." In the ultimate tribute, Green confessed that the bag is so well designed, she herself carries one often.

In summation, Green says, "Shopping bags are walking billboards . . . they build recognition. If it's a wonderful bag, you *will* carry it until it gives out . . . and people *will* notice."

Shopping Bag Title:	**Barney's New York, Shopping Bag Program**	Handle Type:	**Ginger—Twisted paper, Black—Die Cut**
Establishment:	**Barney's New York, New York, NY**	Special Finishing:	**Ginger—Heat Stamped Matte Black, Black—Heat Stamped Matte Silver**
Designer:	**Jenny Barry/Julie Reifler/ Nancye Green**		
Firm:	**Donovan & Green, New York, NY**		
Distributor:	**Modern Arts Packaging, New York, NY**	The textures and soft cord handles contributed strongly to the success of these seemingly simple bags. Incorporation of engineering specifications and market research	
Materials			
Paper:	**Ginger—Leatherette, Black—Deerskin**		

Alex Lindsay
MODERN ARTS PACKAGING

"Graphic competition for the attention of the human eye is tremendous today. If you haven't managed your graphic design properly, you're wasting a lot of advertising money . . . and losing a lot of potential exposure."

According to Alex Lindsay, "Design has always been the KEYSTONE of our business." Design may be the keystone of the *business,* but the key to Lindsay himself is integrity. Lindsay cares, on a very personal level, about the quality of the work he produces. The best design in the world is nothing without this commitment to excellence.

Lindsay, to a certain extent, inherited an interest in shopping bags. His father worked for two major shopping bag manufacturers during his business career. Eventually, Lindsay was hired by one of these companies. He then moved to another, similar company. The new position required him to call on "every small mom-and-pop store in Manhattan." It is a tribute to his love for and interest in shopping bags that he stuck it out.

One of the trends he observed during this period was the tendency to use "wallpaper" packaging. "Wallpaper" was the first major step beyond the plain brown bag for many small stores. The idea was for a bag manufacturer to produce large quantities of several basic patterns on bags and boxes. The salesman's task was to sell one of these patterns to a retailer and imprint the retailer's name and logo on this background.

In the mid-60's, the wallpaper trend backfired. The British influence had engendered such complex designs that the logos often were lost against a backdrop of grey "Glen plaid" or "regimental stripes."

Modern Arts Packaging is a very specialized turn-key operation. It produces shopping bags and other packaging items and design projects from concept through production. Larger conventional orders are produced in the United States. Many specialized productions are done in Central America, Korea, in plants where hand finishing is possible. Modern Arts remains involved from production through delivery to the client. It is this kind of attention to detail which keeps Modern Arts' clients faithful. These clients include many of the European retailers that have stores in the United States such as Charles Jourdan, Yves St. Laurent, and Louis Vuitton, as well as leading American retail stores like Barneys New York, Talbots, and The Gap. Museums such as the Metropolitan Museum of Art and the Whitney Museum of American Art are also premium clients. Modern Arts Packaging does not cater to the middle-of-the-road retailer.

"When asked, we say that we specialize in shopping bags. We produce and coordinate gift paper, printed tissue and ribbon and boxes, but if you throw too many 'specialties' at a client, he tends to become confused. If I'm going to be filed away under one category, I want that category to be 'Shopping Bags'."

Lindsay feels that graphic design for shopping bags is a very specialized genre. "You're not dealing with a perfect manufacturing process; the client must be made aware of what to expect and what *not* to expect." Because of the specialized nature of the work, most of the sales staff are graphic designers and work on the concept as well as the ultimate execution and manufacturing process.

"Cosmetic companies (which provide more than 40% of Modern Arts' work) often do their own creative work." Modern Arts then refines, translates and executes the graphic design into a

Shopping Bag Title:	G. F. is New!
Establishment:	G. F. Furniture Systems, Inc., Chicago, IL
Designer:	Mark Randall
Art Director:	Massimo Vignelli
Firm:	Vignelli & Associates, New York, NY
Distributor:	Modern Arts Packaging, New York, NY
Materials	
Paper:	White Kraft
Coating:	Laminated
Handle Type:	Soft Cord
Special Finishing:	Hang Tag Affixed to Handle

These literature carry bags are part of an image rebuilding program for an 85-year-old furniture company. The message wraps completely around the bag, drawing the eye to explore the full 360-degree rotation.

manufactured reality.

"We encourage our clients to emphasize their store's name and logo on their packaging. It's both a symbol for the customer and a referral for new business." "The shopping bag has emerged as a primary advertising tool during the past five years; its use in that medium has exploded."

"The Modern Arts logo goes on our work. For me, it is a symbol of the care that went into the work. For the customer, it is a guarantee of quality."

Shopping Bag Title:	Jean Patou Christmas '86
Establishment:	Jean Patou, New York, NY
Designer/Art Director:	Janice Brill
Firm:	Janice Brill, Inc., New York, NY
Distributor:	Modern Arts Packaging, New York, NY
Materials	
Paper:	Coated
Coating:	Matte Finish on Lamination
Handle Type:	White Silk with Gold Metallic
Special Finishing:	Rotogravure

The Christmas shopping bag for this manufacturer/distributor of toiletries is exquisitely simple. The couturier's name and home-base city are imprinted in gold foil against a white-on-white pattern of his name. High-gloss laminate coating makes the effect difficult to reproduce in a photograph. In reality, the effect of understated elegance is unmistakable.

Shopping Bag Title:	L'Animale
Establishment:	L'Animale, Englewood, NJ
Designer/Art Director:	Mindy Waters
Firm:	Modern Arts Packaging, New York, NY
Illustrator:	Mindy Waters
Distributor:	Modern Arts Packaging, New York, NY
Materials	
Paper:	White Kraft
Coating:	Laminated
Handle Type:	Black Soft Cord
Special Finishing:	Gold Heat Stamp

The original bag for this women's clothing boutique used lettering executed in an animal print that was not readily legible. However, using the animal print for the entire bag works well. It's a vivid image and a bit of a visual pun. The animal theme print appears on hang tags, business cards, the store's interior and other collaterals.

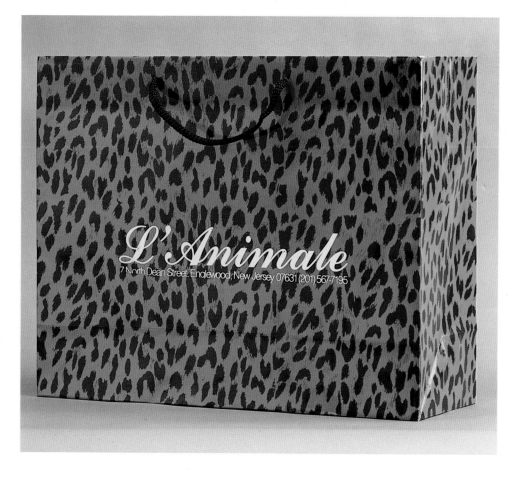

John Jay
Vice President and Creative Director
Bloomingdale's, **New York, NY**

The fact that each bag is different, yet is always recognized as a Bloomingdale's bag, destroys a lot of myths about corporate identity. I *do* see the bags as a means of corporate identity.

No one who is involved with graphic design in America needs an introduction to Bloomingdale's shopping bags. They are famous for their innovative design and for their non-use of the store's name. Though, as Jay notes, "the number one rule about corporate identity is consistency, the consistency of Bloomingdale's shopping bag design is its inconsistency. By reaching past design cliches to the innovative spirit of the art, Jay has helped Bloomingdale's to achieve a unique corporate identity. His success has been achieved because of several factors.

"It all comes down to solving a problem and making sure that the solution fits the problem. Our approach to shopping bag design works for us because it is consistent with the personality of the store. The essence of Bloomingdale's corporate identity has been the absence of a pattern. This is a difficult image to pull off; it will not work for every establishment. Consistently minimalist and austere bags featuring our store logo used year after year would not work for us. It would betray the essence that makes Bloomingdale's unique. Bloomingdale's willingness to take a risk has always been our trademark."

"We have a different kind of personality. There is a certain point of view that characterizes Bloomingdale's—adventurous, constantly changing." The shopping bag design reflects these aspects of the store's philosophy. Although not all Bloomingdale's bags are universally popular, "at least it pushes certain buttons and makes you respond, whether you like it or not."

Jay is responsible for a wide variety of projects beyond shopping bags, and many of them evolve simultaneously. "I don't just come in and say, 'Today, we'll design a shopping bag.'" Juggling many projects has given him a holistic approach to his work. "Everything that inspires you should be brought back into your work. I like the element of surprise. Sometimes this means using someone unusual, say an architect such as Michael Graves, to design a shopping bag. Sometimes it's expressed in the sequence of bags we produce each year."

Shopping Bag Title: **India Spring Promotion**
Establishment: **Bloomingdale's, New York, NY**
Creative Director: **John Jay**
Art Director: **David Au**
Firm: **Bloomingdale's, New York, NY**
Illustrator: **Robert Goldstrom**
Distributor: **Equitable Bag, Long Island City, NY**

Materials
Paper: **Clay Coat**
Handle Type: **Black Plastic**

Inspired by a Persian painting ("Prince Offering Wine to His Mistress," collection of Edwin Binney III, Courtesy Museum of Fine Arts, Boston), this bag is typical of the unique approach Jay uses for bag design. Traditional Indian paintings feature a two-dimensional style, but he wanted more depth than was available in the original painting. He therefore had it altered subtlely to create a more modern appearance. The picture now visually "leaps" off the bag and catches the observer's attention.

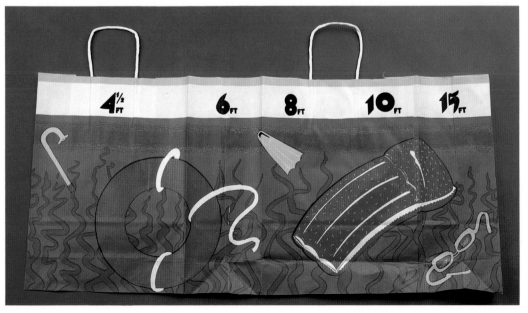

Shopping Bag Title: **Summer Bag**
Establishment: **Bloomingdale's, New York, NY**
Creative Director: **John Jay**
Firm: **Bloomingdale's, New York, NY**
Manufacturer: **Equitable Bag, Long Island City, NY**

Materials
Paper: **White Kraft**
Handle Type: **Twisted Paper**

This bag, designed the previous winter, reduces the summertime objects to a flat, two-dimensional mélange floating in a swimming pool—the ultimate image of summer. The illustration wraps around the bag as the water depth changes and creates a mural effect.

"We do at least five bags each year: New Year's; Spring; Summer; Fall; and Christmas. We may also do special promotions and, of course, the Big Brown Bag is always in use. I like the bags which will succeed one another to contrast well. If the Fall bag will be classical and primarily terracotta in color, then Summer should use vivid colors and perhaps urban street art. The Christmas bag for that year should take yet a third approach."

Some stores *sell* their shopping bags to cover part of the costs; Bloomingdale's never has. "It would be very easy to charge 25¢ to 50¢ per bag. What you would lose is having the maximum number of bags on the street. You'd lose the impact of seeing the bag everywhere. Assuming that people are going to carry shopping bags anyway (and they will), I'd like them to carry ours." Jay has even incorporated the store's shopping bags into ads in other media, citing art exhibits in which they have appeared.

"The most important point in my philosophy about the shopping bag is to get it into as many hands as possible. I see it as an art of the streets. I also want to keep the level of excellence high in terms of its artistic execution. All of this requires a commitment on the part of management. The payoff produced by putting money into shopping bags is not always measurable in a tangible way. Instead, it shows up as prestige, exposure and a reputation for creative excellence."

Shopping Bag Title:	Japan
Establishment:	Bloomingdale's, New York, NY
Creative Director:	John Jay
Art Director:	David Au
Firm:	Bloomingdale's, New York, NY
Illustrator:	Kazumasa Nagai
Calligrapher:	Tim Girvin
Manufacturer:	Equitable Bag, Long Island City, NY
Materials	
Paper:	Clay Coat
Handle Type:	Twisted Paper

Tim Girvin created the logotype for this unusual and vivid bag. John Jay states, "Kazumasa Nagai, one of Japan's premier graphic designers, designed the shopping bag. I wanted to work with someone whose exemplified Japan's international and contemporary design leadership." The store wanted to capture the essence of Japan without resorting to stereotypical design elements. Instead, the rising sun has been split into color bands around the bottom of the bag. If anything, the bag is reminiscent of neon lights in The Ginza, rather than the more pastoral scenes commonly used to represent Japan.

KAZUMASA NAGAI

Bill Weiss
Weiss & Sons,
Glendale, NY

"You've got television, newspapers, radio and packaging . . . the fourth medium."

For Weiss, everything comes back to knowing his immediate customer—the store owner—and the ultimate user—the customer. "Ego, image, desire and competitiveness create the need for a shopping bag. It's advertising . . . keeping the image in front of the public. . . . The customer is the most fun because a customer who gets a bag and loves it advertises the store that provided the bag. . . . It's a mutually profitable arrangement, a good shopping bag. The customer is proud and happy to carry it, and the store is happy to see it on the street."

Weiss' final comment on marketing is both profound and cautionary. "Everybody is out there with a product. Unless you're Con Edison, somebody else can sell the same thing you do. The only way you can do well yourself is if you're willing to go out there and market it. If you don't, someone else will."

Bill Weiss represents the third generation of his family to head this distributorship, which was founded in 1911. The business literally stretches back to a roll of brown paper and a cone of twine. He has grown up with shopping bags and has a bone-deep understanding of how they are designed and what they should do. His first rule is "Know thy customer. Know what he will buy." He views packaging in general as, literally, a fourth medium for advertising.

Although paper bags are generally felt to be the "quality" end of the shopping bag scene, Weiss feels there is a place for plastic, too. "A shopping bag can go from ultra-conservative to ultra-modern. Basically, though, they express one idea, 'What image do I want to present to the people on the street?' "

Shopping Bag Title:	**Spring Street Books**	High-gloss varnish and bright colors
Establishment:	**Spring Street Books, New York, NY**	are not appropriate for every retailer. A woodcut-look black on white
Designer:	**Soo Gunn**	illustration works very well for this
Firm:	**Harry Pincus, New York**	bookstore. The books themselves, and
Distributor:	**Weiss & Sons, Glendale, NY**	the knowledge they contain, are the point. Razzle-dazzle packaging would
Materials		only detract from the message.
Paper:	**White Kraft**	
Handle Type:	**Twisted Paper**	

Shopping Bag Title:	**Foravi**
Establishment:	**Foravi, New York, NY**
Designer:	**Richard Forenza a.k.a. Foravi**
Art Director:	**Richard Forenza a.k.a. Foravi**
Firm:	**Foravi, New York, NY**
Manufacturer:	**Eurobag, Italy**
Distributor:	**Weiss & Sons, Glendale, NY**
Materials	
Bag:	**Plastic**
Handle Type:	**Black Cotton**
Special Finishing:	**Hand-Finished**

This store's speciality, Scandinavian products, is reflected in the geometric design executed in bold primary colors on the white plastic shopping bag. The black fabric handles are affixed in a "shoulder strap" configuration, which permits the shopper to carry home purchases while keeping both hands free.

Shopping Bag Title:	Hamrah's
Establishment:	Hamrah's, Cresskill, NJ
Designer:	Joyce Hamrah
Manufacturer:	Champion International, Walden, NY
Distributor:	Weiss & Sons, Glendale, NY
Materials	
Paper:	Clay Coat
Handle Type:	Plastic
Special Finishing:	Silver Foil Stamped

Foil-stamping and extruded white plastic handles distinguish this cerulean clay coat bag. Though the design is simple, the execution raises it above the ordinary.

"Plastic is very important to the overall bag picture. There are times when it's easier to print on plastic; colors don't become muted—they don't change. The absorbency of paper can change the color you apply. Color matches are much truer with plastic." "The life span of plastic is much longer than that of paper." "On a rainy day, a plastic bag is a wonderful thing."

"It is really awkward to work with designers who don't know production. It is critical to understand what's involved with given equipment and to know what to expect. Offset, trapping problems, screens and color combinations can make or break a design. The designs are often good, but we usually have to modify the design to accommodate the existing equipment." Weiss has, however, worked with numerous creative designers to produce some brilliantly designed bags.

"Price structure and the amount of hand labor required usually determine where a bag will be produced. Salary structures in the United States make it prohibitively expensive to do much hand finishing work here."

Seymour Chwast
Director
Pushpin Studios

"A shopping bag is, in essence, a walking poster. Ideally, the design should be such that it is an *animated* poster."

Co-founder, with Milton Glaser and Ed Sorel, of Pushpin Studios and now director of the influential Pushpin Group, Chwast likes art to be "inventive, but accessible." While satisfying the need to communicate the client's message, he likes to impose an unusual perspective and "follow it where (my) creative curiosity leads me."

In marked contrast to the whimsey of his illustrations, Chwast has a strong preference for conservative typefaces. For shopping bags, he generally prefers uncoated paper, rather than plastic or a glossy-finished stock. "I like the way the ink takes to the paper. There's a 'marriage' between ink and uncoated paper which has a quality that is hidden by coating it."

"Ideally, shopping bags should be designed using a three-dimensional prototype. After all, the bag is not going to be seen folded flat, but in movement." "The best shopping bag designs have the effect of animation . . . a continuous image that extends all the way around the bag will draw the eye better than one which is static in feeling."

"Shopping bags are throwaway art." Chwast feels Andy Warhol's famous Campbell's Soup bag is the classic illustration of the ephemeral nature of the medium. "Warhol began by taking an object that is normally discarded—the soup can—and created art from it. He took the idea to its logical extension by transferring the art *back* to a throwaway object— the shopping bag."

"At best, the shopping bag is a tremendously powerful promotional piece. At least in America, it has essentially replaced both the sandwich board and, often, the poster as a visual selling tool."

Shopping Bag Title:	**Meredith Bag**
Establishment:	**Meredith, Paris, France**
Designer/Art Director:	**Seymour Chwast**
Firm:	**The Pushpin Group,** **New York, NY**
Illustrator:	**Seymour Chwast**
Materials	
Paper:	**Clay Coat**
Coating:	**Laminate**
Handle Type:	**Soft Cord**

This bag was printed in black and white to control production costs. The lettering was designed especially for this bag. The stylized capital "M" reflects the quality of the high-fashion designer clothes carried by the boutique. The Euro-style bag uses a white cord handle for a final touch of elegance.

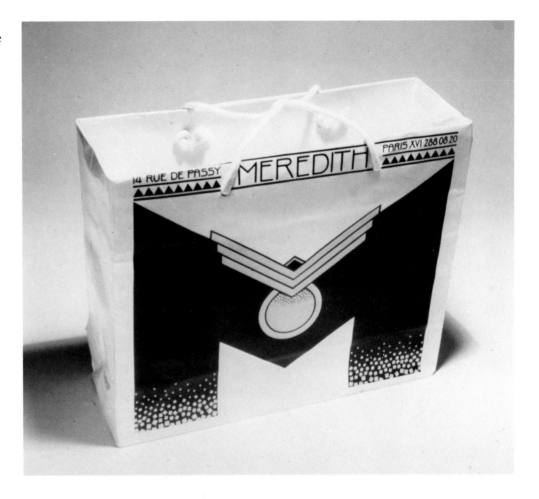

This bag was never produced. Comp shown.

Designer/Art Director:	**Seymour Chwast**
Firm:	**The Pushpin Group** **New York, NY**
Illustrator:	**Seymour Chwast**

Shopping bags and boxes are three-dimensional objects. To take full advantage of the fact that all sides will eventually be seen, the designer has used an animation effect to draw the viewer's eye to additional sides beyond the one first glimpsed. The procession of bicycles is endless, with the front wheel of one becoming the back wheel of the next. This concept makes the shape and use of the shopping bag a design strength, rather than a problem to be resolved.

Metamorphosis

CHAPTER

3

Introduction

Designer shopping bags are so much a part of everyday life, it's hard to imagine a busy street corner without them. Yet the colorful illustrations and varied shapes are relatively recent phenomena. Only 20 years ago, almost all shopping bags were brown or white Kraft paper, with string handles and the store logo as the single design element. A few trend-setters branched out in the early '60's. For the most part, there was little change until about 1972.

A variety of factors contributed to the explosion of creativity which characterized shopping bag design in the 1970's. To understand the phenomenon, however, it is useful to consider the shopping bag in its historical context.

Bandboxes to Bags: 19th to Mid-20th Century

The modern shopping bag has succeeded and replaced the 19th century bandbox—an oval or round container made of pasteboard and equipped with cord straps which could be held in the hand or, more frequently, slipped over the arm. From the standpoint of tensile strength, the bandbox was far superior to the shopping bag. Unfortunately, it was also clumsy and had a tendency to bump against both the bearer and perfect strangers who ventured too close. Bandboxes were also relatively expensive to manufacture and store. Unlike the shopping bag, bandboxes did not collapse for flat storage.

The rise of the basic shopping bag can be traced to several social developments: the decline in the number of servants to support each household, growth of the cities, and increased use of public transportation. Arrival of the private automobile probably finalized the discontinuance of the bandbox. The bandbox survives, in vestigial form, as the modern hat box—hats are too fragile to survive uncrushed in a shopping bag.

The paper used for shopping bags when they were first introduced was not as sturdy as that used today, but the paper didn't need to be. The first generation of shopping bags were only required to hold together long enough to carry purchases from the store to the car and from the car to the house. Reuse of shopping bags, other than for mundane purposes within the home, was rare. Also, until as recently as the 1950's, customers at many of the larger stores also had the option of having even quite small purchases delivered directly to their homes.

The origins of the shopping bag are difficult to trace. It is quite likely that their evolution *parallels* the band-box, rather than descending from that form. Paper bags with tough "wraparound" handles which reinforced the bottoms were used in the early part of this century to transport small quantities of coal or potatoes. As demonstrated in some of the samples published here, the bags were eventually adapted—probably in the late 1920's—to permit easy transport of bottles of soft drinks and beer. Cardboard inserts to separate the bottles minimized breakage. One offshoot of this type of bag was the modern cardboard six-pack carrier.

The customer's perception of the shopping bag as a purely utilitarian object did not begin to shift until the bags themselves changed. When shopping bags became more colorful and varied, a broader range of uses for them began to emerge. Due to factors dictated by the American social scene, the shopping bag eventually evolved into a legitimate art object.

Post-War Art in America

Designer shopping bags are an outgrowth of the post-World War II American art movement. Before the War, American art followed European trends and retained a European perspective on the relative importance of daily life versus the "finer things." American culture was generally perceived, even by Americans, as crude, even vulgar.

America's involvement in World War II, first with the Lend-Lease program and later with actual war activity, restored the country's national pride. Having rolled up their sleeves and thrown the full power of their enormous industrial network into the war effort, Americans began to view their own culture with a new respect. Post-War American art began to glorify the ordinary artifacts of American culture. The free-spending economy of the 1950's, based on the strength and stability of the dollar, gave rise to a tremendous upsurge in consumerism, which led to an increase in advertising. Even the fine arts took on something of the two-dimensional quality of commercial art as expressed in billboards, posters and print ads.

Andy Warhol, Roy Lichtenstein, Robert Rauschenberg, Ray Johnson and others redefined American art. In the early '60's, both Lichtenstein and Warhol took the process one step further. Both chose to use a shopping bag as an art object, creating limited editions of shopping bags with their own art reproduced on this practical object. This was the birth of the shopping bag as a legitimate advertising and art medium. What followed, even the visionary Warhol could hardly have predicted.

A Decade of Change: 1966-1976

Social trends seem to run in 20-year cycles. Decades of creativity and change often alternate with decades of consolidation and stability. The 1920's, for example, was a decade of tremendous social change, expressed in a loosening of rigid standards of social behavior and a tremendous creative surge. The Great Depression of the 1930's necessitated a period of both economic and social retrenchment.

The 1940's, though marred by World War II, again fostered a creative flowering. The 1950's was a decade centered on family and the home. The 1960's was a decade again of change, accelerated through an invention which actually entered the marketplace in the late 1940's—television.

The generation which attained maturity in the 1960's—the earliest crop of what was later described as the "Baby Boomers"—was the first to experience nearly instantaneous mass communication. Coverage of the Free Speech movement at the University of California in 1964, grim footage of the Vietnam War and the image of first landing of man on the surface of the Moon all appeared nightly on the nation's television sets.

Eventually, the national addiction to television created a rebound effect. Young people began to find watching television, rather than experiencing life at first-hand, intolerably suffocating. Thousands set up communes, moved to California or simply took to the roads in an endless search for self identity. One side effect of this movement was an interest in "hands-on" involvement in art. People with little or no formal art training began painting, sculpting and experimenting with light shows— visual presentations keyed to live musical performances.

Other than Lichtenstein and Warhol, few, if any, legitimate artists of the 1960's saw the possibility of translating this revived creativity into shopping bag art. As the '60's ended, however, and the first Baby Boomers entered the work force, mass awareness of the visual arts became an important factor in marketing. The Woodstock generation was intensely involved with color. Men no longer dressed solely in the traditional grey flannel suit, white shirt and conservative tie for business. Instead, pastels, vivid purples and paisley-print ties were the order of the day.

In a society where gaudy plumage was commonplace, a plain white or brown shopping bag was decidedly inappropriate. Gradually, retailers began to experiment with more playful, imaginative imagery in shopping bags. Rampant consumerism provided the impetus for a broader variety of bags.

Partly in response to a rise in foreign travel among the general populace, one of the first appearances of unusual shopping bags was in the promotion of products through "Special Events." Stores began to sponsor sales and special marketing promotions devoted to the cultures and products of foreign, but increasingly-familiar countries. Examples of these bags are presented in the next chapter.

These bags, all drawn from the private collection of E. Marvin Jacobson of Oakland, CA, provide an encapsulated history of the development of the shopping bag from the 1920's to the 1950's.

The "Mission Orange" bag was produced by Triangle Bag Company of Covington, KY, and promotes a California-based soft drink company. Its dyed, twisted paper handles are characteristic of the late 1920's and early 1930's. Even then, the power

of in-gusset printing as an advertising factor was recognized.

The "Moxie" bag from the same period features a whimsical illustration and strong advertising copy. This bag, with its admonition that there are "a hundred later uses," may be the earliest precursor of today's movement to reuse shopping bags. Found in almost pristine condition in Montana, this bag includes cardboard inserts which provided additional strength for the carrier, as well as separated

the individual soft drink bottles to minimize breakage. Although this was the only instance where the separators were found with the bag, it is likely that all such bags employed them.

The "Arrow Beer" bag features unusual flat paper handles with "patent pending" stamped on them. This handle type was not in general usage until the late 1930's. Arrow Beer was a product of Baltimore, MD. No manufacturer is credited on the bag.

DON'T BUY JUDY BOND BLOUSES

- Judy Bond has illegally locked out its workers.
- Judy Bond has illegally refused to bargain with the ILGWU.
- Judy Bond is a "runaway" from a union, with whom it has had a contract for more than a generation.
- Judy Bond has left many skilled workers, who faithfully produced its garments for many years, jobless.

JUDY BOND IS ON STRIKE

INTERNATIONAL LADIES' GARMENT WORKERS' UNION

The Coors carrier bag, circa 1935, features the familiar logo-type and dyed, twisted paper handles. Even then, the company touted its pure Rocky Mountain spring water.

Stegmaier's, of Wilkes-Barre, PA, admonishes customers to "place empty bottles upright," thus ensuring minimal breakage. The copy, which alludes to both bottles and cans, places this bag in the late 1930's. The bag was printed by the Union Bag Company.

Griesedieck Brothers' beer bag has been established as a 1950's artifact by tracing the patent number on the bottom. Developed from a carrier originally designed for fresh produce, its unusual paper handle represents quite a departure from the earlier twisted paper handles, which were secured with heavy-duty staples. The brewery, based in St. Louis, purchased its bags from Package Containers, Inc. of Portland, OR.

The "Don't Buy Judy Bond Blouses" shopping bag represents the earliest use we have found of a "message" bag. Though it's a far cry from the slickly-produced political advertising of today, it is nonetheless the lineal ancestor of current bags promoting political events and individual candidacies. No manufacturer is credited on the bottom of the bag. The only insignia is that of the International Brotherhood of Pulp, Sulphite & Paper Mill Workers. We *do* know the strike took place in Los Angeles in the late 1930's. The shopping bag may have been produced by donated labor in an expression of interunion solidarity. This bag was drawn from the private collection of E. Marvin Jacobson of Oakland, CA.

Shopping Bag Title:	**Trade Show Bag**
Establishment:	**Travel & Leisure Magazine;**
	Division of American
	Express,
	New York, NY
Concept:	**Esther Kaplan**
Firm:	**The Promotion Group**
	Advertising Agency,
	New Jersey
Production:	**Janet Odjis & Company,**
	New York
Manufacturer:	**PAK 2000,**
	Mirror Lake, NH
Materials	
Paper:	**Coated**
Coating:	**Laminate**
Handle Type:	**Soft Cord**
Special Finishing:	**Offset Litho**

This bag, designed as a literature carrier, is unusual for several reasons. The bag was designed to accommodate a specific package of literature—no more and no less. Other companies could not, therefore "piggyback" their literature into the magazine's bag. The thin strips of travel photos tantalize the viewer by providing only part of the story. Sturdy, comfortable, braided-fabric handles encourage the convention-goer to retain the bag.

WALT DISNEY PRODUCTIONS

◄ Shopping Bag Title: Mickey Mouse
Establishment: Burdines, Miami, FL
Designer: Walt Disney/Burdines
Art Director: Burdines
Illustrator: Walt Disney Inc.
Manufacturer: Equitable Bag Company,
Long Island City, NY

Materials
Paper: Clay Coat
Handle Type: Red Plastic

Use of cartoon characters to promote
special events is a growing trend in
the 1980's. Here, in a dual salute to
Disney World and the centennial of
the Statue of Liberty, Mickey Mouse
is featured on a Burdine's shopping
bag. The cooperation of Walt Disney
Productions gave the store a great bag
design; the shopping bag provided
free publicity for Disney World. Such
cooperative ventures are on the rise.

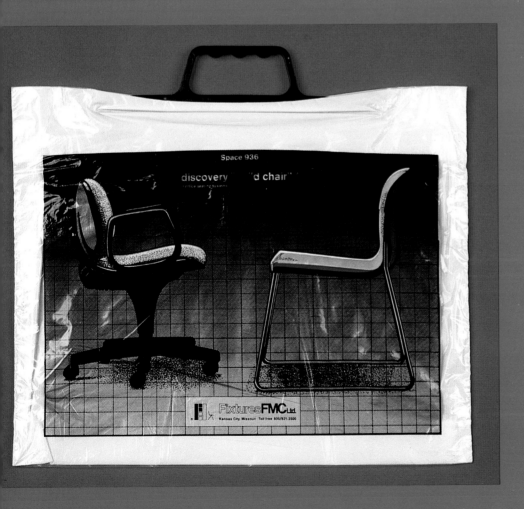

Shopping Bag Title: Discovery/D Chair
Establishment: Fixtures Furniture,
Kansas City, MO
Designer/Art Director: Barry Crone
Firm: Fixtures Furniture,
Kansas City, MO
Photographer: David Ludwigs
Manufacturer: Amko Plastic, Inc.,
Cincinnati, OH
Distributor: The Paper Supply Co.,
Kansas City, MO
Manufacturer: Amko Plastic, Inc.,
Cincinnati, OH

Materials
Bag: Plastic
Handle Type: Plastic

This vinyl bag promoting an office
furniture company uses an unusual
technique to present two new chair
designs. It is an example of a trend
to view shopping bags as a legitimate
advertising medium. A three-color
vinyl overlay is laid over a plain white
vinyl liner. The chairs face one another
to suggest interaction—both of the
furniture and the people who will use
it. They are set against a "high-tech"
silver and black checked background
to convey the sense of a modern
approach to furniture design. The bag
could be used to tote literature either
from the store or from trade shows.

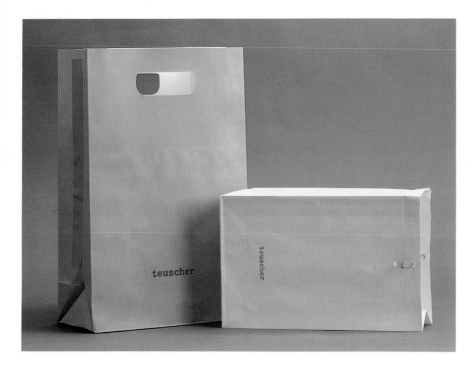

Shopping Bag Title:	**Teuscher**
Store:	**Teuscher Chocolates of Switzerland, San Francisco, CA**
Firm:	**Teuscher Chocolates of Switzerland, Zurich, Switzerland**
Materials	
Paper:	**Kraft**
Special Finishing:	**Ribbon Handle applied after purchase in store**
Handle Type:	**Ribbon**

This retailer of European chocolates varies the colors of its shopping bags to suit the season. Each outlet is independently owned and operated, but all receive their bags from the home office in Switzerland. Each new shipment of bags is a surprise for the store as well as for the customer. In-store decorations change to coordinate with the season's colors. Satin finish ribbon supplies the handle. The logotype remains the same on all bags, but the color of the logo's ink harmonizes with the overall bag color. This attention to detail in coordinating the decorative details, both in the store and on the bags, was unheard of in the 1960's.

Shopping Bag Title:	**Together**	This bag was conceived as a primary advertising tool for a jointly-sponsored charity event. This represents the first such joint effort of a bank and a department store. The bag's design is a visual depiction of the concept as well as a clever pun. The gradual visual approach of the two elements of the coined word eventually results in a gentle overlap. The light, vivid colors give the bag a cheerful quality.
Establishment:	**Emporium-Capwell, San Francisco, CA**	
Designer:	**Jim Frew**	
Art Director:	**John Thomas**	
Firm:	**Emporium-Capwell, San Francisco, CA**	
Distributor:	**Conifer, Berkeley, CA**	
Materials		
Paper:	**Clay Coat**	
Handle Type:	**White Paper**	

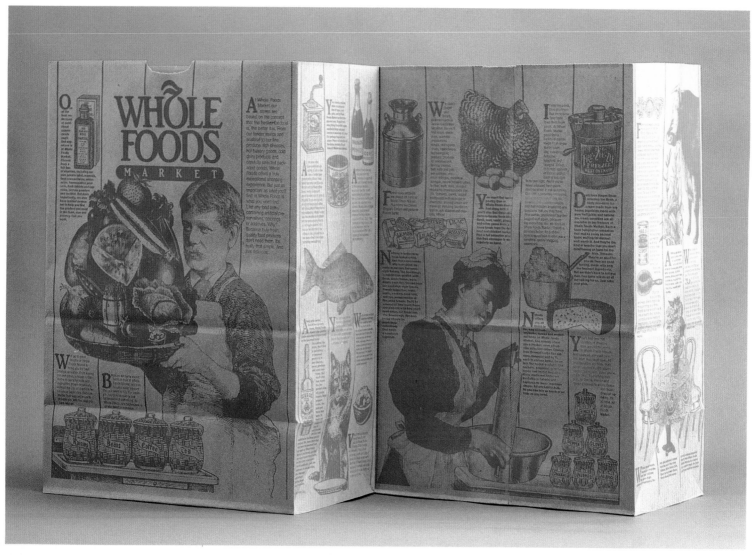

Shopping Bag Title:	**Whole Food Bag**
Establishment:	**Whole Foods Grocery Store, Austin, TX**
Designer:	**Mike Hicks**
Art Director:	**Dave Shapiro**
Firm:	**HIXO, Inc., Austin, TX**
Illustrator:	**Melissa Grimes**
Manufacturer:	**Champion International, Walden, NY**
Materials	
Paper:	**Kraft**

The Whole Foods Market carries a full line of gourmet food items. Unfortunately, in recent years, the word "whole," when used in association with any food-related word, has come to mean health foods and vitamins. To dispel this mistaken idea about the Market, the artist used illustrations of hams, fish, pastry, cheese and condiments on the bag. The brown screening on brown Kraft paper and the choice of turn-of-the-century human figures lend the bag an aura of quality and reliability.

Shopping Bag Title:	**Fresh Plus**	
Establishment:	**Fresh Plus Grocery,**	
	Austin, TX	
Designer:	**Mike Hicks**	
Art Director:	**Tom Poth**	
Firm:	**HIXO Inc., Austin, TX**	
Illustrator:	**Larry McEntire**	
Manufacturer:	**Manville**	
Materials		
Paper:	**Kraft**	

This grocery bag—literally illustrated with grocery items—was created to aid in a store's transition. Originally set for a "Mom and Pop" market, Fresh Plus decided it needed to appeal to a younger audience. The new focus is underlined by the pictures of fresh produce, gourmet items and exotic condiments on the bag. The consistency of the image is ensured by using the same illustrations for in-store signage.

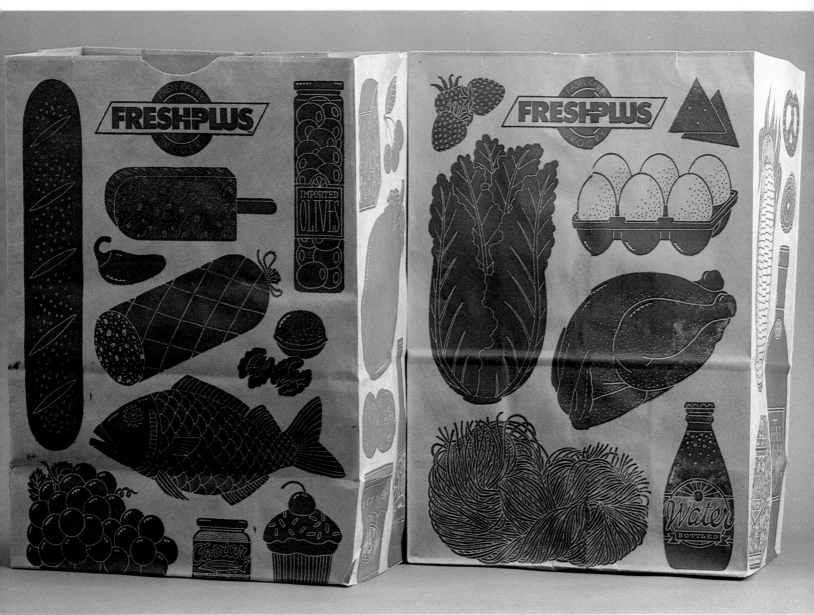

Shopping Bag Title: **British Fortnight 1973**
Establishment: **Neiman-Marcus, Dallas, TX**
Designer: **John Lyons Jr.**
Art Director: **Michaels Matthews**
Firm: **Neiman-Marcus, Dallas, TX**
Illustrator: **Kip Lott**
Manufacturer: **Equitable Bag Company, Long Island City, NY**
Materials
Paper: **Clay Coat**
Handle Type: **Twisted Paper**

This bag cleverly captures a sense of two very different places with a deceptively simple design. The state of Texas is depicted with the center of the British flag superimposed. This image, in turn, becomes the suggested shoulders of a saluting Beefeater. Though the Fortnight is identified on the bag, the designation is hardly needed because of the strength of the visual image.

Shopping Bag Title: **King Tut**
Establishment: **Emporium-Capwell, San Francisco, CA**
Materials
Paper: **Clay Coat**
Handle Type: **Twisted Paper**

The store provided major corporate sponsorship for this highly successful "King Tut" exhibit at San Francisco's De Young Museum. In addition to funding, Emporium-Capwell handled ticket sales and provided space for the associated lectures. Since tickets to this exhibit were as popular as those to major sporting events, the store was able to capitalize on its involvement with a commemorative bag. The bag depicts the exquisite death mask from the tomb of Tutankhamon.

Shopping Bag Title:	**Museum of Modern Art 50**
Establishment:	**The Museum of Modern Art, New York, NY**
Designer:	**Tom Geismar**
Art Director:	**Tom Geismar**
Firm:	**Chermayeff & Geismar Associates, New York, NY**
Manufacturer:	**Continental Extrusion, Garden City, NY**
Materials Plastic	
Handle Type:	**Plastic**

Designed to commemorate the museum's 50th anniversary, this bag is appropriately modern in design. The numerals appear as simple geometric shapes fully assembled in the lower left corner of the bag. Progressing upward and to the right, the numerals are disassembled into their component geometric parts. The geometric sequence, displayed in vivid and sunny primary colors, suggests that the next 50 years may be as unpredictable and exciting for the museum as the first 50 years.

Shopping Bag Title: **Christmas 1978**
Establishment: **Burdine's, Miami, FL**
Art Director: **Charles Senseman**
Firm: **Burdine's, Miami, FL**
Materials
Paper: **Clay Coat**
Handle Type: **Twisted Paper**

When this bag was developed for the 1978 holiday season, Burdine's was seeking an image that was traditional, yet in keeping with its Florida location. The decision was made to use Henri Rousseau's mystical paintings with lush jungle settings. The wonder and mystery of the season are inherent in the dreamy, moonlit sky. The foliage is reminiscent of the Florida landscape. Traditional snow scenes would not have worked nearly as well. Pictures of snow would have remained just that—pictures—if seen against a Florida background.

Shopping Bag Title:	1960 Christmas (Camel Bag)
Establishment:	Neiman-Marcus, Dallas, TX
Art Director:	Art Shipman
Firm:	Neiman-Marcus, Dallas, TX
Illustrator:	B. Kliban
Manufacturer:	Duro Bag, Ludlow, KY
Materials	
Paper:	Clay Coat
Handle Type:	Twisted Paper

Camels laden with brightly-colored bundles march around the bottom of this cheerful bag. Santa Claus is almost lost in the procession. Designed for Christmas of 1960, the bag is a remarkable early departure from the holiday bags of the era, which relied heavily on repeat patterns and traditional colors printed on uncoated Kraft. The bag was designed as a tie-in with that year's featured "His and Hers" gifts in the Neiman-Marcus catalog—a pair of live camels.

Shopping Bag Title:	Waldenkids/Learning Center for Children
Establishment:	Waldenbooks, various locations
Designer:	Dawn Kimmins
Art Director:	Martin Roberts
Firm:	Landor Associates, New York, NY
Illustrator:	Dawn Kimmins
Manufacturer:	Equitable Bag Company, Long Island City, NY
Materials Paper:	Clay Coat
Handle Type:	Red Plastic

This bag is an interesting indicator of two important trends of the 1980's: the tendency to create a shopping bag that is an architectural extension of the store, and the Baby Boomers' sudden, late interest in reproducing themselves. In the past several years, there has been a recent rise in the birth rate. Accordingly, there is a greater market for toys, games and other materials which make learning fun. Waldenkids supplies such products. The shopping bag, part of a coordinated identity program, uses the three basic shapes a child first recognizes, and colors drawn from a basic crayon set to communicate its message. Employee pins, signage, gift stickers and wrapping paper are other elements in this imaginative program. The design appeals to parents and children alike.

Shopping Bag Title:	**Summer Inside/Out (Caribbean)**
Establishment:	**Conran's, New York, NY**
Designer/Art Director:	**Betty Chow**
Firm:	**Conran's Design Group, New York, NY**
Illustrator:	**Betty Chow**
Manufacturer:	**Champion International, Walden, NY**
Materials	
Paper:	**White Kraft**
Handle Type:	**Twisted Paper**

In marked contrast to the shopping bags of earlier eras, the bag of the 80's covers the entire surface with color. This bag, in celebration of summer, uses both an indoor and an outdoor visual. The "in" side face is set against a cheerful striped wall; the "out" side features summer flowers and foliage against a deep blue sky. The bag name switches from top to bottom to enhance the feeling of movement and energy.

Shopping Bag Title:	**Generation**
Establishment:	**Liberty House, Honolulu, HI**
Designer/Art Director:	**Heather A. Chun**
Firm:	**Liberty House, Honolulu, HI**
Illustrator:	**Royden Seiki**
Distributor:	**Paul Steinbroner/Packaging Consultant Inc., Manhattan Beach, CA**
Manufacturer:	**Equitable Bag Company, Long Island City, NY**
Materials	
Paper:	**Clay Coat**
Handle Type:	**Cloud Grey Plastic**

This shopping bag reflects the current trend to incorporate elements of in-store architecture in the shopping bag design. The pebbled background of the bag is drawn directly from the interior design of Liberty House's junior department, "Generation". The bright pastels, geometric shapes and staggered type reflect the department's youthful orientation.

Shopping Bag Title:	**Bonwit Teller Packaging**
Establishment:	**Bonwit Teller, New York, NY**
Designer:	**Gene Grossman**
Firm:	**Anspach Grossman and Portugal Inc., New York, NY**

The store's "bunch of violets" is one of the oldest decorative images in designer shopping bags. This bag represents the most recent update of the familiar pattern. More impressionistic in feeling than earlier versions, this one is softer and more feminine, yet continues to evoke the familiar, dependable image. More traditional renderings are used for the associated packaging, which includes tissue paper and gift boxes as well as smaller bags. This is a good example of how enduring images may change slightly over time to reflect changes in the popular culture.

Special Events

CHAPTER

4

Shopping bags have significantly changed over the past two decades. Once, creating a special bag for the mid-winter holiday season was a major undertaking. Now, a store may develop a bag in connection with the opening of a new outlet or sponsor as many as five or six special events during the year.

Often, these "special event" bags are designed or illustrated by noted artists. Almost invariably, they are finely constructed and produced. More than a special sales promotion is involved. These bags promote a specific image, and a certain style on which the store can capitalize for the balance of the year.

Shopping Bag Title:	**Hello Hong Kong**
Establishment:	**Seibu Department Store, Tokyo, Japan**
Designer:	**Alan Chan/Alvin Chan**
Art Director:	**Alan Chan**
Firm:	**Alan Chan Design Company, Wanchai, Hong Kong**
Materials	
Handle Type:	**Plastic**

East meets West in this colorful bag designed for a fair celebrating Hong Kong held in a major Japanese department store. The word "hello" appears in English; the ideograms below say "Hong Kong". On the reverse, the dragon's tail was produced in traditional Chinese brush painting; his head was generated on a computer.

Shopping Bag Title: **Tradewell Grand Opening Bag**

Establishment: Tradewell Group, Renton, WA

Designer: Jack Anderson, Julie Tanagi

Art Director: Jack Anderson

Firm: Hornall Anderson Design Works, Seattle, WA

Distributor: Food Services of America, Kent, WA

Manufacturer: Princeton Packaging, Tacoma, WA

Materials

Paper: **Kraft**

This high-end food market revamped its logo concurrently with remodeling its premises. The Grand Opening was a reopening with a subtle change in emphasis. The muted colors used for the confetti and the new logo lend a certain distinction to the plain brown Kraft bag. The bag was the introductory use of the new logo. The associated bags used within the market feature the logo in dark type, with the confetti pattern executed in two to three soft colors.

Shopping Bag Title: **Imagine a Store . . . Macy's Fresno**

Establishment: Macy's California, San Francisco, CA

Designer: Fortunato Fong

Art Director: Richard Nodine

Firm: Fong & Associates Design, San Francisco, CA

Illustrator: Fortunato Fong

Printer: A.G.I., Chicago, IL

Manufacturer: Champion International, Walden, NY

Materials

Paper: **Clay Coat**

Finishing: **Electron Beam**

Handle Type: **Twisted Paper**

When Macy's California opened its new store in Fresno, a strong sense of place was needed. Fresno is located in the heart of the richest agricultural land in California, possibly in the world. Endless orange groves and vast vineyards characterize the area. At the same time it is a sophisticated business community. The bag celebrating the store opening gracefully captures these disparate elements.

Shopping Bag Title:	**Shoes Wow**
Establishment:	**Burdines, Miami, FL**
Illustrator:	**Heimstra**
Manufacturer:	**Equitable Bag Company, Long Island City, NY**
Materials	
Paper:	**Clay Coat**
Handle Type:	**Plastic**

Burdines produces a special event twice a year. In addition to a shopping bag, coordinated direct mail and television ads are prepared. The pattern here is composed of shoes, the star of the event. Though this bag uses colors and images which are different from those of the store's signature bag, the design of the bag remains consistent with Burdines uniquely Floridian image. The gussets provide information via horizontally-set type once the face of the bag has caught the eye.

Shopping Bag Title:	Progetto Italiano
Establishment:	Nordstrom, Seattle, WA
Designer:	Tim Girvin, Seattle, WA
Art Director:	Cheryl Fujii
Firm:	Nordstrom Advertising, Seattle, WA
Illustrator/ Calligrapher:	Tim Girvin
Printer:	A.G.I., Chicago, IL
Manufacturer:	Champion International, Walden, NY
Materials	
Paper:	Clay Coat
Coating:	Electron Beam
Handle Type:	Custom Silver Plastic

The designer has used a loosely sketched Italian flag as the backdrop for the bag title. The stylized calligraphy and the impression of movement embodied in the flag emphasize the excitement and forward-thinking trends of today's Italian fashions. The fashion theme is further delineated by the fabric look of the bag itself. The bag name is prominently displayed in Italian. The translation appears discreetly reversed in white, next to the Nordstrom name.

Shopping Bag Title:	**Japan '85**
Establishment:	**Weinstock's, Sacramento, CA**
Designer:	**P. K. Kirtley**
Art Director:	**Marianita Howard**
Firm:	**Weinstock's, Sacramento, CA**
Photographer:	**David Robbin**
Printer:	**A.G.I., Chicago, IL**
Manufacturer:	**Champion International, Walden, NY**
Materials	
Paper:	**Clay Coat**
Coating:	**Electron Beam**
Handle Type:	**Twisted Paper**

A Japanese girl adorned with traditional make-up and hair ornaments is the main illustrative image in this bag. To represent Japan's high-tech aspects, she sports a contemporary, rather than traditional, hair style. What she is wearing below the neck is a mystery, also appropriate vis à vis a westerner's view of Japan. This promotion was jointly sponsored by the store and the American Express Company. American Express' involvement is acknowledged in the bag gussets.

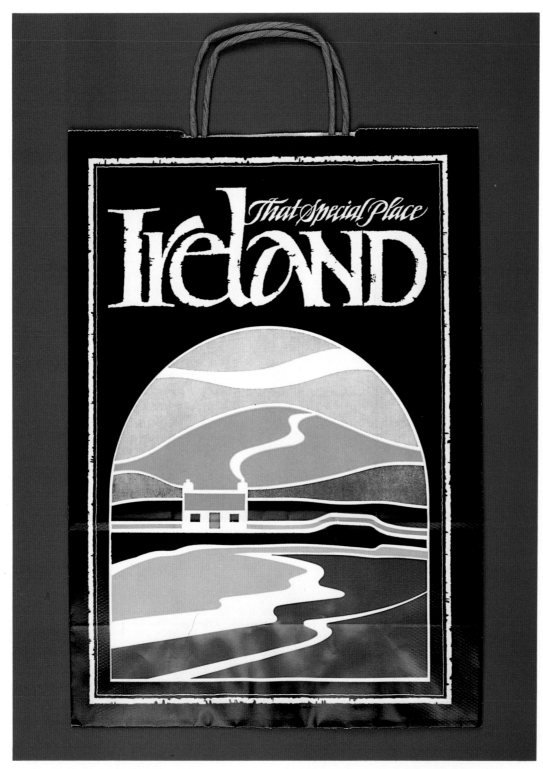

Shopping Bag Title: **China** ▶
Establishment: **Bloomingdale's,**
New York, NY
Creative Director: **John Jay**
Firm: **Bloomingdale's,**
New York, NY
Manufacturer: **Champion**
International,
Walden, NY
Materials
Paper: **White Kraft**
Handle Type: **Twisted Paper**

It is relatively easy to produce art depicting China from a westerner's point of view. Depicting China as the Chinese see it is more difficult—and more interesting. The design for this bag was the winner of a competition held in Beijing and Shanghai, where contests are very rare. The artist has chosen to represent the Great Wall in a violet landscape with a red sky. Since the Chinese associate the color red with happiness, this is a very cheerful bag!

Shopping Bag Title: Ireland . . . that Special
Place
Establishment: Bloomingdale's,
New York, NY
Creative Director: John Jay
Firm: Bloomingdale's,
New York, NY
Manufacturer: Equitable Bag Company,
Long Island City, NY
Materials
Paper: Clay Coat
Handle Type: Twisted Paper

Produced for a country promotion highlighting Irish products, this bag was also designed in Ireland. A competition was held in Dublin to obtain the basic design. The peaceful cottage nestled between hills and a river is both the traditional image of the country and a contemporary reality.

Shopping Bag Title: **South China Seas**
Establishment: **Bloomingdale's,**
New York, NY
Designer/Illustrator: **Tim Girvin, Seattle, WA**
Creative Director: **John Jay**
Firm: **Bloomingdale's,**
New York, NY
Manufacturer: **Duro Bag, Ludlow, KY**
Materials
Paper: **Clay Coat**
Handle Type: **Twisted Paper**

The artist used a loose brush stroke
to write the names of the countries
featured in the gussets. Color was
applied batik fashion to create the
atmosphere of southeast Asia for
this bag. Colorful, image-filled, and
bursting with life, the bag reflects
the culture well. One side depicts a
stylized rendition of the formal temples
of Bangkok. The other side reflects the
beaches and lush wildlife of Bali.

Shopping Bag Title:	**Italian Fortnight 1975**	The broad-brush splashes of red and green against a white background pay homage to the energy and imagination of modern Italian graphics. The importance of the visual imagery is highlighted by providing the verbal description in discreet outline, white against black.
Establishment:	**Neiman-Marcus, Dallas, TX**	
Art Director:	**Richard Nelson**	
Firm:	**Neiman-Marcus, Dallas, TX**	
Manufacturer:	**Equitable Bag Company,**	
	Long Island City, NY	
Materials		
Paper:	**Clay Coat**	
Handle Type:	**Twisted Paper**	

Shopping Bag Title: **Japan Fortnight 1974**
Establishment: **Neiman-Marcus, Dallas, TX**
Art Director: **Richard Nelson**
Firm: **Neiman-Marcus, Dallas, TX**
Materials
Paper: **Clay Coat**
Handle Type: **Twisted Paper**

Images of Kabuki actors and Samurai warriors drawn from 19th century woodcuts invoke the Japanese culture on this bag. The color scheme and grid pattern subtly illustrate both the variety and orderliness of Japanese society.

Shopping Bag Title:	Australian Fortnight 1986-87
Establishment:	Neiman-Marcus, Dallas, TX
Designer:	Kemper Johnson
Art Director:	Michaels Matthews
Firm:	Neiman-Marcus, Dallas, TX
Illustrator:	Karen Helm
Printer:	A.G.I., Chicago, IL
Manufacturer:	Champion International, Walden, NY
Materials	
Paper:	Clay Coat
Coating:	Electron Beam
Handle Type:	Twisted Paper

Australia has become the chic vacation destination in the '80s. The kangaroos in sunglasses on this bag reflect the excitement and growth of Australia as a tourist attraction. The world-famous Sydney Opera House and Ayers Rock serve as a backdrop for rollicking marsupials. Neiman-Marcus has captured the immediacy and excitement of Australian culture in this bag for one of its famous "Fortnights."

Shopping Bag Title:	**By the Sea . . . France**
	Fortnight 1985
Establishment:	**Neiman-Marcus, Dallas, TX**
Designer:	**Steve Miterko**
Art Director:	**Michael Matthews**
Firm:	**Neiman-Marcus, Dallas, TX**
Illustrator:	**Mark Langeneckert**
Printer:	**A.G.I., Chicago, IL**
Manufacturer:	**Champion International,**
	Walden, NY
Materials	
Paper:	**Clay Coat**
Coating:	**Electron Beam**
Handle Type:	**Twisted Paper**

The tranquility of a French fishing
village is portrayed in the pointillist
style of George Seurat on this bag. The
vivid interplay of the various dots of
color lends depth to the illustration.
Electron beam coating provides the
finishing touch for this elegant bag.

Holiday Bags

CHAPTER

5

In the yearly "life" of a retail establishment, special occasions and holidays are the high watermark in sales. However, at Christmas, Easter, Valentine's Day and other major holidays, competition is fierce for the customer's dollar. In order to distance itself from its competitors, a store will strive to produce the best, and oftentimes most nostalgic or inventive, holiday bag it can afford.

Holidays evoke emotional memories in the average individual. A store can help increase its sales during these periods by offering shopping bags displaying images that appeal to the customer's emotions.

As with many special bags, holiday bags must be ordered nearly six to eight months in advance. The ability to forecast the trends likely to be popular in a given season, well in advance, is, therefore, highly prized.

Shopping Bag Title: **Christmas Joy 1981**
Establishment: **Neiman-Marcus, Dallas, TX**
Art Director: **Michael Matthews**
Firm: **Neiman-Marcus, Dallas, TX**
Manufacturer: **Equitable Bag Company, Long Island City, NY**

Materials
Paper: **Clay Coat**
Handle Type: **Twisted Paper**

The illustration on this bag was based on a cartoon cell purchased from Walt Disney studios, and was designed to coordinate with the store's famous Christmas catalog. Animation was a major theme for the catalog that year, 1981, and Mickey Mouse and his pals enjoying the camaraderie of the season projected a festive and loveable holiday bag message.

Shopping Bag Title: **Christmas 1983 Hirschfeld Bag**
Establishment: **Neiman-Marcus, Dallas, TX**
Design Firm: **Neiman-Marcus, Dallas, TX**
Illustrator: **Al Hirschfeld**
Materials
Paper: **Clay Coat**
Handle Type: **Twisted Paper**

In a radical departure from his usual style, Al Hirschfeld used poster paints rather than the more familiar pen and ink to produce the illustration for this bag. Santa cavorts with pipes and bell through snow flurries against a midnight blue sky. If you can find the "Nina" (the name of Hirschfeld's daughter, and his personal, private "joke" incorporated into his artworks), more power to you. We couldn't. Simple clay coated paper and twisted paper handles support the fantasy of the illustration.

Shopping Bag Title: **Christmas 1984**
Establishment: **Neiman-Marcus, Dallas, TX**
Designer/Art Director: **Bob Halliday**
Firm: **Bob Halliday, Minneapolis, MN**
Illustrator: **Willa Langheimer**
Printer: **A.G.I, Chicago, IL**
Manufacturer: **Champion International, Walden, NY**

Materials
Paper: **Clay Coat**
Coating: **Electron Beam**
Handle Type: **Twisted Paper**

Artist Willa Langheimer's popular Christmas postcard has been reworked on stretched canvas and translated into this Christmas shopping bag. The bag relies on the combination of whimsy and nostalgia for its success. A serene blue sky and white snow serve as the backdrop for the topiary holly balloon with its unusual passengers. Electron beam coating enhances the appearance of the finished bag.

Shopping Bag Title: **Our Holiday Heritage**
Establishment: **Nordstrom, Seattle, WA**
Designer: **Julie North**
Art Director: **Cheryl Fujii**
Firm: **Nordstrom Advertising, Seattle, WA**
Illustrator: **Rob Kemp**
Calligrapher: **Tony Kimball**
Printer: **A.G.I, Chicago, IL**
Manufacturer: **Champion International, Walden, NY**

Materials
Paper: **Clay Coat**
Coating: **Electron Beam**
Handle Type: **Tan Plastic**

For the 1985 holiday season, Nordstrom's design staff created a fabric for use with in-store displays. The fabric pattern, Scandinavian and outdoor in feeling, is repeated on the associated shopping bag. In the gussets, a well-conceived message appropriate to the season appears. The bag is designed to be appropriate for any mid-winter holiday, including Christmas and Hannukkah.

Shopping Bag Title: **A Time of Traditions**
◀ Establishment: **Nordstrom, Seattle, WA**
Designer: **Kim Foster**
Art Director: **Cheryl Fujii**
Firm: **Nordstrom Advertising, Seattle, WA**
Photographer: **Howard Fry and Jill Sebella (Hand Tinting)**
Printer: **A.G.I, Chicago, IL**
Manufacturer: **Champion International, Walden, NY**

Materials
Paper: **Clay Coat**
Coating: **Electron Beam**
Handle Type: **Twisted Paper**

A hand-tinted photograph of the traditional '80's family on a winter holiday adorns this very non-traditional Christmas bag. Only the typeface is typical of Christmas packaging. The bag is, however, a successful marketing piece. The family seems happy to be in the winter wonderland the art director fashioned for them—and they're all clad in the upscale sportswear Nordstrom carries.

Shopping Bag Title: **Sunny Bunny**
Establishment: **Emporium-Capwell, San Francisco, CA**
Designer: **Joe Hong—Sunny Art**
Art Director: **John Thomas**
Firm: **Emporium-Capwell, San Francisco, CA**
Distributor: **Hirsch Enterprises, San Francisco, CA**
Material
Handle Type: **Pullstring rope**
Bag: **Plastic**

This shopping bag was designed especially to accommodate Sunny Bunny, a value-added promotion for Easter 1987. Normally retailing for $20.00, the toy was $10.00 with a minimum $25.00 purchase during a spring sale which culminated in an associated charity benefit. Ten outsized Sunny Bunnies were donated to charitable organizations specializing in assistance to children.

Shopping Bag Title:	"C's Illuminated"
Establishment:	**Emporium-Capwell, San Francisco, CA**
Designer:	**Carlos Marchioni**
Distributor:	**Conifer, Berkeley, CA**
Materials	
Paper:	**Clay Coat**
Handle Type:	**Twisted Paper**

The artist used the letter "C" in a whimsical series of illustrations to portray images associated with the holiday season. The squared illustrations are reminiscent of children's blocks. The images include bells, dolls, candy canes, a reindeer and Mr. Claus himself, rushing off to deliver the Christmas goodies.

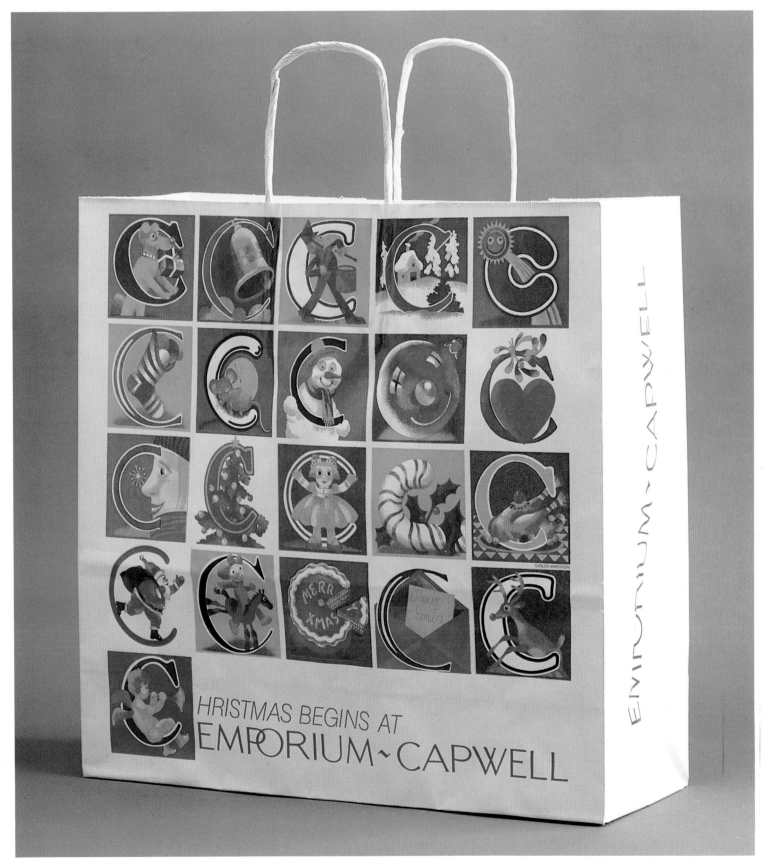

Shopping Bag Title:	**Jingle Bear**
Establishment:	**Emporium-Capwell,**
	San Francisco, CA
Designer:	**Ray Cruz**
Art Director:	**John Thomas**
	(Emporium-Capwell)
Firm:	**Vicki Morgan Associates,**
	New York, NY
Distributor:	**SPS Company Packaging**
	Consultants, Los Angeles, CA
Materials	
Handle Type:	**Pull-String Rope**

As a value-added incentive, the store introduced "Jingle Bear" for the 1986 holiday season. The bear appeared on the shopping bag, was available at special "Polar Station Outposts" in the various store branches and had its own story book. The promotion was launched in coordination with a series of breakfasts featuring actors costumed as characters from the Jingle Bear story.

Shopping Bag Title: **1985 New Year's Bag**
Establishment: **Bloomingdale's, New York, NY**
Designer/Illustrator: **Tim Girvin, Seattle, WA**
Creative Director: **John Jay**
Firm: **Bloomingdale's, New York, NY**
Manufacturer: **Champion International, Walden, NY**
Materials
Paper: **White Kraft**
Handle Type: **Flat Paper**

Bloomingdale's has produced a special New Year's bag each year since 1981. It's a clever marketing technique. Customers welcome a change of pace from the ever-lengthening commercial Christmas season. The New Year's bag offers a visual lift in January, the midpoint of the winter season. End of the year sales and January white sales keep the "walking billboard" on the street for several weeks. This particular bag pays homage to the influence of architecture on that year's design.

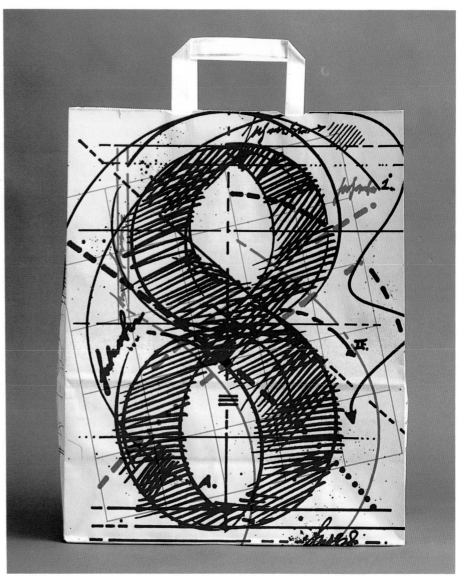

Shopping Bag Title:	**Art of Giving—Snoopy**
Establishment:	**Weinstock's, Sacramento, CA**
Designer/Art Director:	**P. K. Kirtley**
Firm:	**Weinstock's, Sacramento, CA**
Illustrator:	**Charles Schulz**
Distributor:	**Armor Paper Products, Los Angeles, CA**
Materials	
Paper:	**Clay Coat**
Coating:	**Laminate**
Handle Type:	**Yellow Plastic**

Weinstock's commissioned the illustration used on this bag from Charles Schulz especially for their Christmas promotion. Snoopy's festive clothing, characteristic "dance" and the gifts he bears are all in keeping with the theme of the bag. The cheerful red background and yellow plastic handle are appropriately bright, in keeping with the season. Weinstock's often uses both regionally- and nationally-recognized artists to design their Christmas bags.

Shopping Bag Title:	**Annie Leibovitz/ Willard Scott**
Establishment:	**Dayton Hudson Department Store Company, Minneapolis, MN**
Designer:	**Karen Brown**
Art Director:	**Minda Gralnek**
Firm:	**Dayton Hudson Department Store Company, Minneapolis, MN**
Photographer:	**Annie Leibovitz (feature photo) Andre Eccles (gusset photo)**
Printer:	**A.G.I., Chicago, IL**
Manufacturer:	**Champion International, Walden, NY**
Materials Paper:	**Clay Coat**
Coating:	**Electron Beam**
Handle Type:	**White Plastic**

Willard Scott was the store's celebrity Santa in 1985. Photographer Annie Leibovitz provided an additional celebrity theme for the bags. Whimsey and charm were the keynotes for the visual appeal of the bag; both are reinforced by the exquisite photography, the signatures below the photograph, and the gusset copy.

Shopping Bag Title:	**Fantasy Lady Christmas Bag**
Establishment:	**J. C. Penney Company, Inc., New York, NY**
Art Director:	**James Carver**
Firm:	**J. C. Penney, New York, NY**
Illustrator:	**Ray Porter**
Manufacturer:	**Equitable Bag Company, Long Island City, NY**
Materials	
Paper:	**Clay Coat**
Handle Type:	**Twisted Paper**

This Art Deco Christmas bag, from 1985, represents J. C. Penney's first foray into the fashion-oriented bag market. The overall feeling is sophisticated, yet playful. The candy cane, with bow, is the lady's pigtail. The cylindrical shapes in the design are echoed in the elongated, narrow shape of the bag itself.

Shopping Bag Title:	**Christmas**
Establishment:	**Conran's, New York, NY**
Designer:	**Nicholas Bouyoukas**
Art Director:	**Betty Chow**
Firm:	**Conran's Design Group, New York, NY**
Illustrator:	**Nicholas Bouyoukas**
Manufacturer:	**Champion International, Walden, NY**
Materials Paper:	**White Kraft**
Handle Type:	**Twisted Paper**

This strongly graphic bag presents standard Christmas images—a Christmas tree and wreath—in an unusual way. The colors used are bright without being particularly traditional. A cut paper technique was used to develop the design. In-store banners and wreaths sent from the London branch coordinated with the bag.

Shopping Bag Title:	**Christmas Wish 1984**
Establishment:	**Emporium-Capwell,** **San Francisco, CA**
Designer:	**Ray Cruz**
Art Director:	**John Thomas (Emporium-** **Capwell)**
Firm:	**Vicki Morgan Associates,** **New York, NY**
Distributor:	**Conifer, Berkeley, CA**
Materials	
Paper:	**Clay Coat**
Handle Type:	**White Plastic**

Emporium-Capwell developed a single character—a jolly bear in a Santa Claus suit—for use on its Christmas bags from one year to the next. In the first year, he appeared hugging a laden Christmas tree. To facilitate the coordinated television and newspaper promotions, an animated bear in costume was developed by the Animatronics Division of Lucas Film in Marin County, California.

Shopping Bag Title:	**Christmas Bear 1985 "Nicholas"**
Establishment:	**Emporium-Capwell, San Francisco, CA**
Designer:	**Ray Cruz**
Art Director:	**John Thomas, Emporium-Capwell**
Firm:	**Vicki Morgan Associates, New York, NY**
Distributor:	**Conifer, Berkeley, CA**
Materials	
Paper:	**Clay Coat**
Handle Type:	**White Plastic**

The Christmas bear developed for Emporium-Capwell in 1984 was used again in 1985. In the intervening year, the bear acquired a name—Nicholas—and a young friend. The image presented is warm and joyous. As in the 1984 bag, the colors are vivid and cheerful. The bear's costume has been made to appear softer and more old-fashioned than on the previous year's bag to enhance the traditional feeling.

Shopping Bag Title:	**Christmas 1982**
Establishment:	**Bloomingdale's, New York, NY**
Creative Director:	**John Jay**
Artist:	**Karen Jacobson**
Firm:	**Bloomingdale's, New York, NY**
Manufacturer:	**Equitable Bag Company, Long Island City, NY**
Materials	
Paper:	**Clay Coat**
Handle Type:	**Twisted Paper**

Christmas 1982 followed a major promotion of American products at Bloomingdale's. To maintain the feeling of Americana, the store selected Karen Jacobson, a noted folk painter, to depict two different views of Lexington Avenue at Christmas. The illustrations not only appeared on a shopping bag, but were also used in the Christmas catalog and were sold as a poster in the store.

Shopping Bag Title: **Santabear's First Christmas**
Establishment: **Dayton Hudson Department Store Company, Minneapolis, MN**
Designer: **Karen Brown**
Art Director: **Minda Gralnek**
Firm: **Dayton Hudson Department Store Company, Minneapolis, MN**
Illustrator: **Howard B. Lewis**
Printer: **A.G.I, Chicago, IL**
Manufacturer: **Champion International, Walden, NY**
Paper: **Crystal Coat**
Coating: **Electron Beam**
Handle Type: **White Plastic**

The store's exclusive mascot, Santa Bear, had his own television special during the holiday season. As a tie-in, the special's story line was summarized in words and pictures on the holiday bag. The air time and station were listed in the gussets. Electron beam coating provided a highly-polished finish for the bag.

Packaging Programs

CHAPTER

6

Packaging can involve a broad variety of media—
everything from signage to hang tags to tissue paper
to boxes and shopping bags. But in all instances, it
involves a subtle restatement of an establishment's
basic corporate identity.

Unlike the expression of an identity in stationery
or printed collateral materials, packaging can be
playful. It can, and *should,* deviate just a bit from
the established criteria. It is critical that both
the designer and the retailer remember that, for
the *true* end-user—the customer—shopping is a
recreational activity. As such, it should be fun. The
packaging should promote this concept.

Shopping Bag Title: **Chinese Arts & Crafts**
Establishment: **The Chinese Arts & Crafts (HK) Ltd., Kowloon, Hong Kong**
Designer: **Alan Chan/Benjamin Lau**
Art Director: **Alan Chan**
Firm: **Alan Chan Design Company, Wanchai, Hong Kong**
Materials
Handle Type: **Rope and Die-Cut**

Chinese products form the major portion of this store's stock. Granite is used extensively in the store's interior. The designer chose to highlight both in the shopping bags, using a granite-textured background for the upper portion of the bags, with a reversed ideogram. The ideogram appears on the lower half in the granite pattern. Coordinated wrapping paper is gray, with ideograms and their English translations in muted colors.

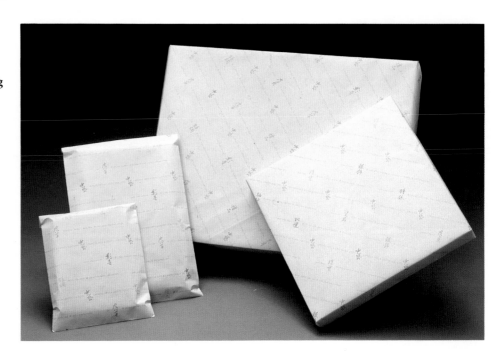

Shopping Bag Title:	**Larimer Square Building Bag**
Establishment:	**Larimer Square Associates, Denver, CO**
Designer:	**Gail Slatter**
Art Director:	**Christina Weber**
Firm:	**Weber Design, Denver, CO**
Distributor:	**B & B Distributing Company, Denver, CO**
Manufacturer:	**Equitable Bag Company, Long Island City, NY**
Materials	
Paper:	**Clay Coat**
Handle Type:	**Twisted Paper**
Special Finishing:	**Gloss Varnish**

Larimer Square is a restored block of landmark buildings which have been adapted for a blend of office and retail spaces. This bag, aimed at the tourist market, features a wraparound illustration of the buildings as they appeared at the turn of the century. A subdued color scheme contributes to the period feeling of the bag. Identifying the location as Denver in the logo enhances the memento value of the piece.

Shopping Bag Title:	**Macy's Shopping Bags**
Establishment:	**Macy's California,**
	San Francisco, CA
Designer:	**Fortunato Fong**
Art Director:	**Richard Nodine**
Firm:	**Fong & Associates Design,**
	San Francisco, CA
Distributor:	**Conifer, Berkeley, CA**
Manufacturer:	**Equitable Bag Company,**
	Long Island City, NY
Materials	
Paper:	**Clay Coat**
Handle Type:	**Twisted Paper**

The main shopping bag uses
rectangular blocks of color against a
grey rectangle to suggest the broad
variety of goods available in the stores.
The grey rectangle is, in turn, set
against a grid, suggesting an organized
approach. For the associated
packaging—boxes and smaller bags
in a wide range of sizes—each color
used on the main bag appears as a
single square or rectangle set against
a variant of the basic grid. In all cases,
the Macy's name is reversed in white
against the color. The clay coated
paper and simple handles lend a clean
look to the design.

◀ Shopping Bag Title: **Larimer Square Angel Bag**
Establishment: **Larimer Square Associates, Denver, CO**
Designer: **Gail Slatter**
Art Director: **Christina Weber**
Firm: **Weber Design, Denver, CO**
Distributor: **B & B Distributing Company, Denver, CO**
Manufacturer: **Equitable Bag Company, Long Island City, NY**
Materials
Paper: **Clay Coat**
Handle Type: **Twisted Paper**
Special Finishing: **Gloss Varnish**

This bag, aimed at the local market, used a bronze statue in the Square as its inspiration. The angel, a familiar landmark to locals, appears on cloth book bags, mugs and tee shirts as well as the shopping bag. The steel etching used in the illustration and a classic typeface contribute a period feeling to the design.

Shopping Bag Title: **Facere Jewelry Art**
Establishment: **Facere Jewelry Art, Seattle, WA**
Designers: **Jack Anderson/Juliet Shen**
Art Director: **Jack Anderson**
Firm: **Hornall Anderson Design Works, Seattle, WA**
Illustrator: **Bruce Hale**
Manufacturer: **Richmark, Seattle, WA**
Materials
Paper: **Dull, Silver Foil**

More contemporary in feeling than its sister store, Facere Jewelry Art specializes in designer jewelry art. The jewelry is also somewhat less expensive. The colors used in the packaging are drawn from the store's interior. Stick-on labels provide a high-tech touch. Coordinated tissue paper lends a note of sophistication.

Shopping Bag Title: **Chickery Take-out Bag**
Establishment: **Dayton Hudson Department Store Company, Minneapolis, MN**
Designer/Art Director: **Robert Valentine**
Firm: **Dayton Hudson Department Store Company, Minneapolis, MN**
Illustrator: **Robert Valentine**
Manufacturer: **Duro Bag, Ludlow, KY**

The Chickery, a take-out restaurant located in the upscale Dayton-Hudson Department Stores, sells only chicken-based dishes. The packaging captures the essence of the restaurant by using a chicken, an egg and a "squiggly" arrow to suggest speed. Because the stores wanted to convey the notion that fast food need not be unhealthy or unappealing, the package design is festive and tasteful. The design is repeated on a broad range of package types.

Shopping Bag Title: **The Chocolate Truffle**
Establishment: **The Chocolate Truffle, Denver, CO**
Designers: **Christina Weber/Gail Slatter**
Firm: **Weber Design, Denver, CO**
Distributor: **Zellerbach Paper Company, Denver, CO**
Materials
Paper: **Clay Coat**
Special Finishing: **Gloss Varnish**
Handle Type: **Twisted Paper**

This gourmet chocolate shop markets only house-made chocolate. It wanted a blend of whimsey and sophistication for its logo. The word "truffle," in its formal script, provides the sophistication. The "chocolate," designed to resemble the script on the kind of chocolate bar you break into pieces, whimsically 'wraps' the truffle. Tissue paper used in the store matches the blue used for the word "truffle." The logo also appears on boxes and in the store's signage. The chocolate letters appear suspended near the ceiling of the store and are repeated, painted on the floor. Their most delicious use, though, is as five-inch long blocks in the store's chocolate alphabet.

Shopping Bag Title:	A. I. Friedman Shopping Bag
Establishment:	A. I. Friedman Inc., New York, NY
Designer:	Willi Kunz
Art Director:	Willi Kunz
Firm:	Willi Kunz Associates Inc., New York, NY
Illustrator:	Eli Kince
Manufacturer:	Contemporary Packaging Corporation, Plainview, NY
Materials Plastic	
Handle Type:	Die-Cut

Originally developed for divider pages in a product catalog, these clean, precise images illustrate the stock of this quality art and drafting supplies store. The tools depicted are reduced to severe, elegant outlines. The bag escapes somberness through the vivid red stripe down one side.

Shopping Bag Title:	**Facere**	Muted colors drawn from the store's interior were used in the bags and boxes for this high-end jewelry store. Purchasing jewelry should always make the customer feel special. To this end, coordinated ribbons and silk flowers adorn the boxes and bags. At the same time, the gently curved geometric shapes in the overall pattern provide a dreamy quality to the design.
Establishment:	**Facere, A Jewelry Salon, Seattle, WA**	
Designer:	**Jack Anderson/Cliff Chung**	
Art Director:	**Jack Anderson**	
Firm:	**Hornall Anderson Design Works, Seattle, WA**	
Illustrator:	**Bruce Hale**	
Distributor:	**Paper Specialties, Seattle, WA**	

Shopping Bag Title: Avant

Establishment: Avant, Minneapolis, MN

Designer: Chuck Spencer Anderson

Art Director: Chuck Spencer Anderson

Firm: Duffy Design Group, Minneapolis, MN

Illustrator: Chuck Spencer Anderson

Materials

Bag: Plastic

Handle Type: Die-Cut

The shopping bag for this fashionable hair salon was deliberately executed in black and white. The idea was to maintain a consistent image with the products, but not to overpower them. The same silhouette that appears on the bag is executed in electric colors against a dramatic black background on each of the individual hair care products.

Shopping Bag Title:	**Savories**
Establishment:	**Savories, New York, NY**
Client:	**Restaurant Associates**
Designers:	**Tom Geismar/**
	Susan Schunick
Art Director:	**Tom Geismar**
Firm:	**Chermayeff & Geismar**
	Associates, New York, NY

Savories is an upscale take-out restaurant that features foods strictly American in derivation. Since most people associate American cuisine with a casual atmosphere, and a somewhat elegant feeling was sought, this presented an interesting design challenge. The solution was to use the needlework sampler, both American in feeling and elegant, as a design motif. The sampler styling, and crisp green and white color scheme give the bags and boxes a neat, finished look.

Shopping Bag Title: **InfoWorks**
Establishment: **Dallas Market Center, Dallas, TX**
Designer/Art Director: **Woody Pirtle**
Firm: **Pirtle Design, Dallas, TX**
Manufacturer: **Equitable Bag Company, Long Island City, NY**

Materials
Paper: **White Uncoated**
Handle Type: **Twisted Paper**

A bold black image, ranging from a studied architectural step design at one end to a broad brush stroke at the other, is the focal point of this design. The shopping bag, used to carry literature from this contract furniture market, was only one element in the overall image. Coordinated pieces ranging from brochures to fabric banners in the buying area were executed in the same yellow, black, red and blue color scheme.

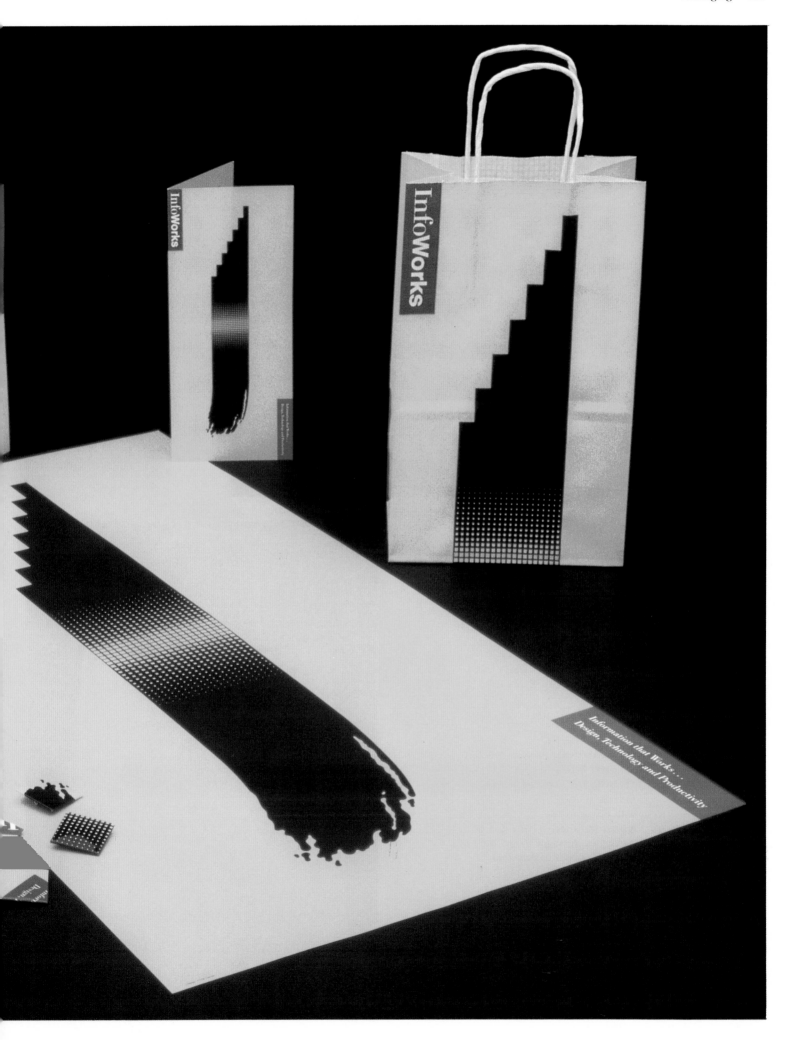

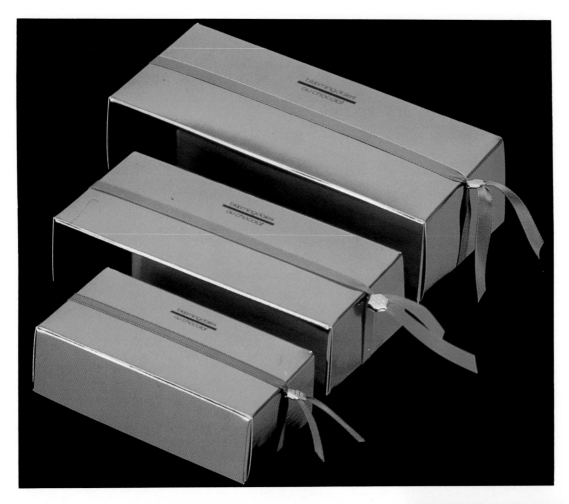

Shopping Bag Title: **Au Chocolat**
Establishment: **Bloomingdale's,
New York, NY**
Designer/Art Director: **Robert P. Gersin**
Firm: **Robert P. Gersin Associates
New York, NY**
Manufacturer: **Equitable Bag Company,
Long Island City, NY**

Materials
Paper: **Clay Coat**
Coating: **Varnish**
Handle Type: **Expresso/Poly Flex**

Chocolate is festive, especially French
chocolate. The packaging for this line
of speciality food products reflects
the sheer luxury of a gift of chocolate.
The reflective copper boxes have vivid
ribbons in very feminine colors, affixed
with tiny gold seals. The shopping bags
feature the same ribbons, in exuberant
"squiggles" to suggest celebrations,
against a copper background.

Shopping Bag Title:	Hold Everything Bag & Box
Establishment:	Hold Everything/Williams Sonoma, San Francisco, CA
Designers:	John Bricker, Alicen Armstrong
Art Director:	John Bricker
Firm:	Gensler Graphics Group, San Francisco, CA
Photographer:	David Wakely
Distributor:	Vanguard Papers, San Leandro, CA
Manufacturers:	Champion International, Walden, NY
Materials	
Paper:	Coated
Handle Type:	White Plastic

Hold Everything sells organizers designed to do just that—hold everything. The store's name is therefore an important element in the packaging design. The image sought was consistency and organization. Use of primary colors and a coordinated grid system further this concept. All of the bags feature one of the colors drawn from the four-color logo in the word "Hold." In addition to the shopping bag, there are boxes, gift cards and a book bag. The boxes feature the four-color logo and use color-coordinated ribbon and tissue paper.

Shopping Bag Title:	**Perrins**	The simple image of a growing plant highlights Perrin's devotion to natural foods prepared for carry-out convenience. The two-color design can be reversed, enlarged or reduced for variety. The same design is used in stationery and food containers.
Establishment:	**Perrins Delicatessen, Minneapolis, MN**	
Designer/Art Director:	**Charles Spencer Anderson**	
Firm:	**Duffy Design Group, Minneapolis, MN**	
Illustrator:	**Charles Spencer Anderson**	
Materials		
Paper:	**Speckletone French**	
Handle Type:	**Twisted Paper**	

Shopping Bag Title:	**Chow**
Establishment:	**Chow Catering, Dallas, TX**
Designer/Art Director:	**Linda Eissler**
Firm:	**Eisenberg Inc., Dallas, TX**
Calligrapher:	**Linda Eissler**
Manufacturer:	**Sample House, Dallas, TX**
Materials	
Paper:	**White Kraft**
Handle Type:	**Twisted Paper**

The packaging for this catering company was developed based on the corporate logo. The designer knew the budget was limited and that the logo would be the easiest place to start. The simple geometric shapes are printed in bright colors against a black strip. This design is festive, yet legible. Because the packing containers vary widely in size and shape, the logos are printed on matte finish label paper via offset lithography. To ensure a consistent look, match colors are specified.

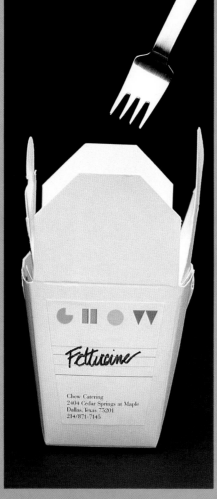

Specialty Bags

CHAPTER

7

In general, shopping bags promote retail establishments. When they are employed as an advertising medium outside their "natural habitat," the observer tends to stop and take notice. It is this element of surprise which permits museums, symphonies, public relations firms and others to use shopping bags as a legitimate and effective advertising medium.

Specialty bags may also employ unusual materials or designs—features uniquely suited to the nontraditional uses to which they are applied. A symphony may use a "non-rustling" type of plastic for its shopping bags to minimize mid-performance disturbances. Gift bags, designed to be used in lieu of wrapping paper, are also a growing trend. Shopping bags are infinitely adaptable and, in "Specialty Bags," their versatility is most evident.

Shopping Bag Title: **Peace on Earth**
Designer: **Mary Engelbreit**
Art Director: **Elaine Cumiskey**
Firm: **The Stephen Lawrence Company, Carlstadt, NJ**
Distributor: **The Stephen Lawrence Company, Carlstadt, NJ**
Materials
Paper: **Printed Offset**
Coating: **Plastic Laminate**
Handle Type: **Black Cotton Cord**

Christmas holly wreathes around the lion and the lamb, both bundled up against winter's chill. Though the image is strongly Biblical, whimsy prevents the religious overtones from overwhelming the recipient of this gift bag. Vivid inks and superior printing make this bag a package to save and reuse.

Shopping Bag Title:	**Believe**	Christmas packaging often evokes memories of childhood holidays— cookies, warm kitchens, family and, of course, Santa Claus. A 19th century Santa is represented here. Images of stars, hearts and crescent moons on his sack of toys lend a mystical quality to the illustration. The festive packaging actually becomes a part of the gift.
Designer:	**Mary Engelbreit**	
Art Director:	**Elaine Cumiskey**	
Firm:	**The Stephen Lawrence Company, Carlstadt, NJ**	
Distributor:	**The Stephen Lawrence Company, Carlstadt, NJ**	
Materials		
Paper:	**Printed Offset**	
Coating:	**Plastic Laminate**	
Handle Type:	**Yellow Cotton Cord**	

Shopping Bag Title:	**Word of Mouth**
Establishment:	**Word of Mouth,** **New York, NY**
Designer/Art Director:	**Roger Whitehouse**
Firm:	**Whitehouse & Company,** **New York, NY**
Illustrator:	**Anon**
Manufacturer:	**Champion International,** **Walden, NY**
Materials	
Paper:	**White Kraft**
Handle Type:	**Twisted Paper**

The simple image of the mouth in brown mezzotint on white Kraft paper is a visual pun. Word of Mouth is an exclusive gourmet food shop. Its clientele is select; the way one finds out about the shop is by word of mouth. Nowhere on the bag do the name and address of the store appear.

Shopping Bag Title:	**People**
Establishment:	**People Magazine, Time Inc., New York, NY**
Designer:	**Liza Greene (bag design)**
Art Director:	**Sanae Yamazaki (cover design)**
Firm:	**People Magazine, New York, NY**
Distributor:	**Promotion Group, Tenafly, NJ**
Materials	
Paper:	**Coated**
Coating:	**Laminated**
Handle Type:	**Soft Cord**

These full-color laminated bags are as slick and involving as the magazine they promote. The bags are used at trade conventions in lieu of booths. They are less expensive than a booth and, at the same time, more practical and fun. The design for the bag is simple—each bag features a different magazine cover. The woven propylene handles make the bags comfortable to carry, even when they are used to transport relatively heavy objects, such as the literature handouts common at trade conventions.

Shopping Bag Title: **Color**
Establishment: **Xerox Corporation, Rochester, NY**
Designer/Art Director: **James L. Selak**
Creative Director: **Tom Saffen**
Firm: **Xerox Corporation, Fairport, NY**
Illustrator: **James L. Selak**
Manufacturer: **Collett Printing Company, Division of A.B. Cowles, Victor, NY**
Materials
Paper: **Uncoated White Offset Vellum**
Handle Type: **Snap'n Carry**
Coating: **Clear Varnish**

This bag is designed to promote the Xerox 350 color slide system and the 6500 color copier at large trade shows. At the top of the bag, a dual image of the word 'color' is presented in vivid orange and peach against a bright blue background. Gradually, from the top of the bag to the bottom, the word is disassembled visually, as the colors become progressively lighter. The effect reduces the typography to simple geometric shapes, and suggests that color copying may be a simple solution to complex marketing presentation problems.

Shopping Bag Title: **Domaine Chandon's Gift Bags**
Establishment: **Domaine Chandon, Yountville, CA**
Designer: **Reesa Shore**
Distributor: **Zellerbach Paper Co., San Francisco, CA**
Manufacturer: **Continental Extrusion Corp., Garden City, NY**
Materials
Bag: **Plastic**
Handle Type: **Plastic**

The design for Domaine Chandon's shopping bags and gift boxes is based on the label for its most famous product—Domaine Chandon Brut, a Napa Valley sparkling wine. Made via the méthod champenoise, it is California's answer to the champagne made by the parent company, Möet et Chandon of France. The "Monet star," which appears in outline on the bottle label, is stamped in gold foil on the gift boxes, and appears in repeat pattern executed in gold ink against a deep green panel on the white plastic bags. Two handle types are used: rigid black plastic tubing for the smaller bag, and a broad smooth white handle on the larger. The smooth handles contribute to the customer's comfort when transporting two or more bottles of wine.

Shopping Bag Title:	**New York Philharmonic**
Establishment:	**New York Philharmonic, New York, NY**
Distributor:	**Weiss & Sons, Glendale, NY**
Materials Bag:	**Plastic**
Handle Type:	**Die-Cut**

The orchestra's logo—New York City nestled in the curve of a French horn—is repeated on this shopping bag used in Philharmonic Hall's gift shop. Because patrons frequently shop before performances, and carry their purchases into the hall, a relatively "noiseless" plastic was chosen as the bag material. The contrast of matte and glossy inks lends the bag a note of sophistication.

Shopping Bag Title:	**Lake Scene in Zurich**
Establishment:	**Teuscher Chocolates of Switzerland, New York, NY**
Designer:	**B. Bloom**
Firm:	**Teuscher Chocolates of Switzerland, New York, NY**
Illustrator:	**Taken from a 1915 Swiss poster by famous Swiss poster artist, O. Baumberger.**
Distributor:	**Alpha Color Graphics, Flushing, NY**
Materials	
Paper:	**Clay Coat**
Coating:	**Laminate**
Handle Type:	**Soft Cord**

Swiss chocolate is famous for its quality. No "hard sell" image would be half as effective as this scene by poster artist, O. Baumberger, evocative of a simpler, more gracious time. The thick (and therefore, more comfortable) handle provides the final touch of quality.

Shopping Bag Title:	**Just Desserts**
Establishment:	**Just Desserts,**
	San Francisco, CA
Designer/Art Director:	**Primo Angeli**
Firm:	**Primo Angeli Inc.,**
	San Francisco, CA
Distributor:	**Unisource, Dublin, CA**
Manufacturer:	**Amko Plastic,**
	Cincinnati, OH
Materials	
Bag:	**Plastic**
Handle Type:	**Plastic**

This small chain is devoted to making delicious desserts—fudgy brownies, blondies, opulent cakes and good coffee are their mainstays. The butterscotch and chocolate color scheme of their bag underlines this point. Practicality (some of these desserts are "gooey") dictated use of plastic rather than paper. The simple, stylized cake in the logo reflects the fact that all desserts are made in-house with the finest ingredients.

Shopping Bag Title:	**Metropolitan Museum of Art**
Establishment:	**Metropolitan Museum of Art Bookstore, New York, NY**
Designer/Art Director:	**Rudolph de Harak**
Firm:	**De Harak & Poulin Associates, New York, NY**
Manufacturer:	**Equitable Bag Company, Long Island City, NY**
Materials Paper:	**Kraft**
Handle Type:	**Twisted Paper**

Classic typography and brilliant colors distinguish these eye-catching bags. The design seems straightforward, but uses an interesting visual technique to achieve its success. The type is large enough to be read from across a busy street. The name of the museum wraps completely around the bag. Even though the viewer probably knows what the name is, the eye is persuaded to follow and read the wrapped image in movement to be sure.

Shopping Bag Title:	Museum of Modern Art Gift Shop
Establishment:	Museum of Modern Art, New York, NY
Designer:	Takenobu Igarashi
Art Director:	Takenobu Igarashi
Firm:	Igarashi Studio, Tokyo, Japan
Materials	
Bag:	Plastic
Handle:	Flat Plastic

This bag extends a design theme projected on the previous MoMA gift bag. The museum's image had been built on a bag featuring distinctive, orderly, circular patterns. A more modern design was sought which retained the circles because of their established and intense identification with the museum. The solution is an elegant, tightly-knit design which incorporates dots into a pattern reminiscent of computer circuitry. The sleek black plastic handles contribute to the high-tech effect. The museum's name appears in white on the black background in a solid sans-serif typeface at the bottom of the bag.

Shopping Bag Title:	**King Kong**™	In addition to producing and distributing films, Universal Studios offers tourists one of the best studio tours available. Visitors experience earthquakes, tropical storms, western shoot-outs and even the parting of the Red Sea. This souvenir bag, sold at the Studio's gift shop, commemorates famous stars from the studio's films, both past and present. What better way to present them than cupped in the hand of the biggest star of them all—King Kong! The hand-affixed, flat-braid cord handles and high-gloss varnish make the vivid red bag a special memento of a day spent amid fantasies made real . . . at least for the moment
Establishment:	**Universal Studios, Universal City, CA**	
Concept:	**Claude Roessiger and David Brown from PAK 2000, with John Poorman from Universal Studios**	
Designer/Artist:	**Mick McGinty**	
Manufacturer:	**PAK 2000, Mirror Lake, NH**	
Materials		
Paper:	**Coated**	
Coating:	**Laminate**	
Special Finishing:	**Offset Litho** .	
Handle Type:	**Soft Cord**	

The old-time country doctor and nurse, reminiscent of Clara Barton's era, evoke the warm and caring qualities of hospital professionals. The image is strengthened further by the field of flowers and small child in the foreground. By varying the scale of the images and making the doctor and nurse larger than the house, child and flowers, the artist has emphasized the medical professionals as protectors of home, nature and children. The bag, printed in one color on brown Kraft paper, is used to carry small items home from the hospital.

Shopping Bag Title:	**Hendrick Medical Center**
Establishment:	**Hendrick Medical Center, Abilene, TX**
Designer/Art Director:	**Duana Gill**
Firm:	**Hixo, Inc., Austin, TX**
Illustrators:	**Duana Gill/Janice Ashford**
Distributor:	**Creative Retail Packaging, Inc., Kingwood, TX**
Materials	
Paper:	**Kraft**
Handle Type:	**Twisted Paper**

Shopping Bag Title:	**The Licensing Stars of the 80's**
Establishment:	**King Features, New York, NY**
Designer:	**Beth Firmin**
Art Director:	**Grant King**
Firm:	**King Features, New York, NY**
Distributor:	**Weiss & Sons, Glendale, NY**
Manufacturer:	**Bag Craft**
Materials	
Bag:	**Plastic**
Handle Type:	**Die-Cut**

These plastic bags with die-cut handles are designed to carry literature collected at animators' conventions. The characters here underline the increasing tendency to use cartoon characters—identified icons of our culture—as motifs on shopping bags.

Shopping Bag Title:	Pop! Pop! Popcorn!
Establishment:	All Cineplex Odeon North American theatres, including Plitt, RKO Century Warner, Neighborhood and SRO, Toronto, Ontario, Canada
Designer:	Lawrence Ayliffe
Firm:	Ayliffe & Allience, Toronto, Ontario, Canada
Manufacturer:	DRG Packaging, Inc., Toronto, Ontario, Canada
Materials Paper:	Outer Layer, Stain Resistant Bladepak; Inner Layer, Grease Guard
Special Finishing:	Flexographic Printing

Fresh, hot popcorn with real butter—no substitutes!—is the marketing message projected by this bag. The yellow kernels are clearly visible against the vivid red, stain-resistant outer wrapper. The interior of the bag is lined in grease-proof paper, which allows the bag to remain crisp looking until all its contents are consumed. The theatre chain employees find the bags easier to store than cardboard tubs, and quieter when used in a theatre environment. Note that the "POP! POP!" theme is repeated in both English and French,—appropriate in Canada.

Shopping Bag Title:	**Solomon R. Guggenheim Museum Shopping Bag**
Establishment:	**The Solomon R. Guggenheim Museum, New York, NY**
Designer/Art Director:	**Malcolm Grear**
Firm:	**Malcolm Grear Designers, Providence, RI**
Distributor:	**Bret Packaging, Needham, MA**
Materials	
Paper:	**Clay Coat**
Coating:	**Varnished**
Handle Type:	**White Twisted Paper**

A stylized view of the front elevation of the Museum is a repeated pattern on this bag. Each side of the bag is emblazoned with a red accent. On one side of the bag, red fills one of the patterns; on the other, red is vividly scribbled over a pattern. The bright accent creates a sense of movement, action and immediacy. A glossy varnish contributes a note of sophistication to the bag design.

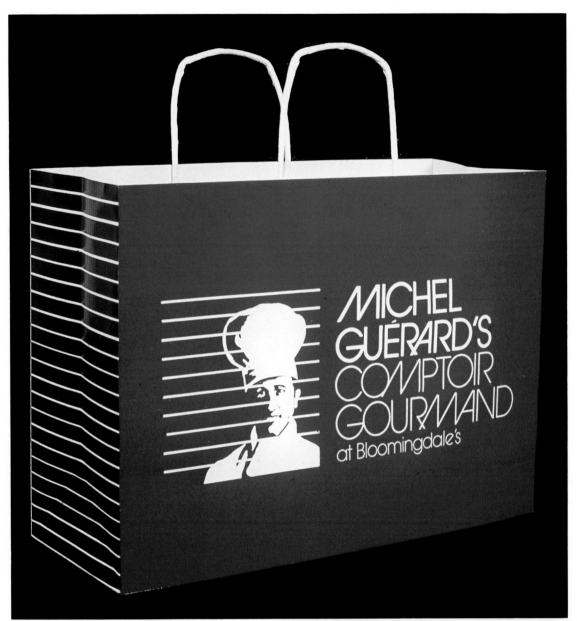

Shopping Bag Title:	**Michel Guerards Comptoir Gourmand**
Establishment:	**Bloomingdale's, New York, NY**
Art Director:	**Robert P. Gersin**
Firm:	**Robert P. Gersin Assoc., Inc., New York, NY**
Manufacturer:	**Equitable Bag Company, Long Island City, NY**
Materials	
Paper:	**Clay Coat**
Coating:	**Varnish**
Handle Type:	**Twisted Paper**

This shopping bag is part of a color-coordinated program which includes wrap-around sleeves for various food containers. Use of the chef's face on each element builds brand awareness and reinforces the message of sophisticated dining. The sleeves are a particularly creative solution to the problem of transferring flat printed promotion or labeling onto a three-dimensional object.

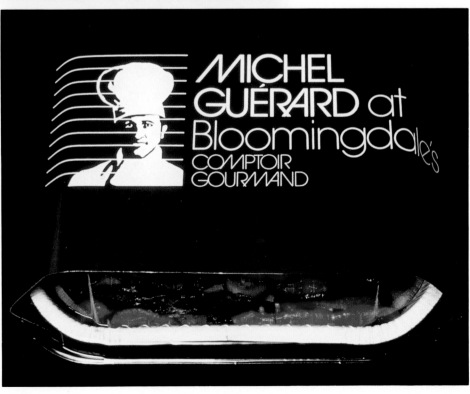

Promotions

CHAPTER

8

Small stores in shopping malls realize sales benefits from the image created by the mall itself. One of the best tools for effecting this type of promotion is a shopping bag promoting the overall image of the mall. Unlike a generalized, "downtown" shopping area, a mall can *choose* which stores will be able to rent space, and reject those which do not conform to the general image.

Another major use of promotional-type bags is the promotion of individual new product lines. The most effective—and visually arresting—of these are the cosmetic bags. These use match colors and sensual images to depict new shades of make-up and lipsticks, for example, in a way best calculated to appeal to their primary customers— women between the ages of 16 and 35. Artistic photography and picture-perfect printing characterize these bags. It is in these promotional materials that the adage noting a picture is worth a thousand words is most vividly realized.

Shopping Bag Title:	**Valley View**
Establishment:	**Valley View Center, Dallas, TX**
Designer:	**Steve Gibbs**
Art Directors:	**Don Sibley/Steve Gibbs**
Firm:	**Sibley/Peteet Design, Dallas, TX**
Illustrator:	**Steve Gibbs, Don Sibley**
Manufacturer:	**Champion International, Walden, NY**
Materials	
Paper:	**Clay Coat**
Handle Type:	**Twisted Paper**

These bags were an integral part of a coordinated collateral/TV/radio/ graphics campaign to upgrade the image of the Valley View Center mall as a fashionable place to shop. The graphic images used on the bags are minimalist, yet sprightly. The image sought was fashion-conscious, youthful and fun. Use of pastels against a black background contributed to the "surprise" factor in this design.

Shopping Bag Title:	**Villa Linda Mall**
Establishment:	**Herring Marathon Group, Dallas, TX**
Designer/Art Director:	**Don Sibley**
Firm:	**Sibley/Peteet Design, Dallas, TX**
Illustrator:	**Don Sibley**
Distributor:	**Creative Retail Packaging, Kingwood, TX**
Materials	
Paper:	**Clay Coat**
Handle Type:	**Twisted Paper**

A stylized, very feminine high-heeled shoe is set against the Santa Fe vista of desert and mountains to give this mall theme bag a definite "sense of place." Santa Fe's artistic sensibilities required that the mall promotion not be jarring, yet a sense of fashion and fun was essential. The design solution was this outrageous shoe, which dominates a background familiar to potential mall customers. To enhance the sense of the familiar, the colors of the desert—at all times of the day—were used on the bag.

Shopping Bag Title:	**The Market Citicorp Center**
Establishment:	**Citicorp, New York; New York, NY**
Designer/Art Director:	**Kiyoshi Kanai**
Firm:	**Kiyoshi Kanai Inc., New York, NY**
Illustrator:	**Kiyoshi Kanai**
Manufacturer:	**Champion International, Walden, NY**
Materials	
Paper:	**Clay Coat**
Handle Type:	**Twisted Paper**

This bag promotes the Atrium shopping area of the Citicorp Center. Spread over three floors, the complex of boutiques and small eating establishments encircles and focuses attention on the Atrium itself. The Atrium's plants, interesting staircases and vast space soften and enhance the architectural impact of the office building above. The artist used the match colors of Citicorp's logo and the well-known silhouette of the building itself to recall the Atrium to the public. The bag was designed so that the silhouette appears to best advantage when the bag is opened to full extension. Ultraviolet coating lends the bag a sophisticated look.

Shopping Bag Title:	**Ken Done**
Store:	**Ken Done,**
	Santa Monica, CA
Designer:	**Ken Done**
Manufacturer:	**Armor Paper,**
	Los Angeles, CA
Materials	
Bag:	**Plastic**
Handle Type:	**Draw String**

Ken Done specializes in textile art—art you can wear and live with in your home. His work has a naive, happy feeling. This is further expressed in his logo in which the sun replaces the "o" in his last name. The vivid colors reproduce well on the plastic bag. This bag and associated logo signage are used in all of Done's Australian stores. The logo will be used in all future stores and in conjunction with new product development.

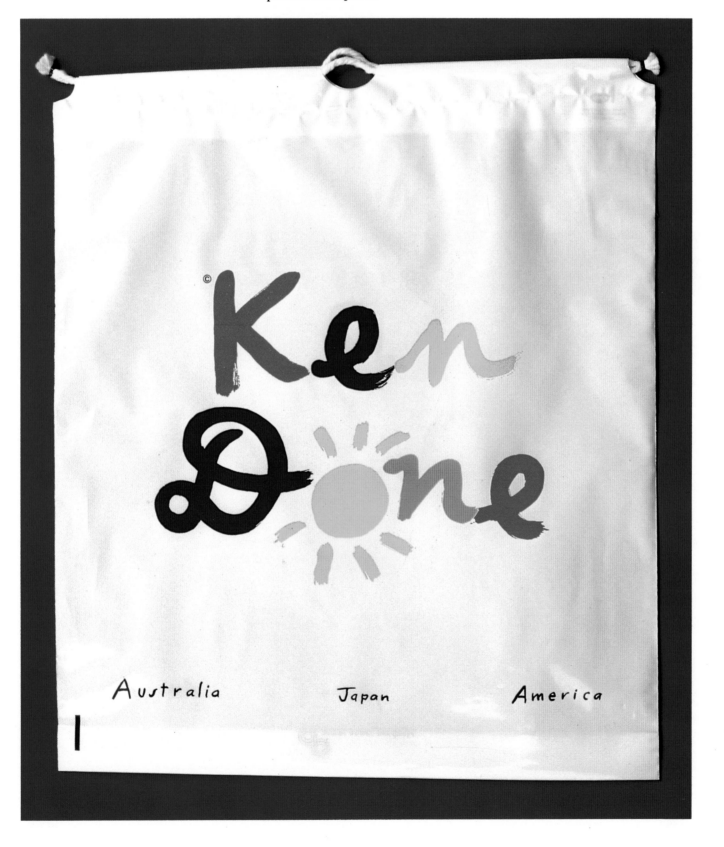

Shopping Bag Title:	**'Pi' Boutique**
Establishment:	**The Copperfield Co. Ltd., Kowloon, Hong Kong**
Designers:	**Alan Chan/Alvin Chan**
Art Director:	**Alan Chan**
Firm:	**Alan Chan Design Company, Wanchai, Hong Kong**
Materials	
Paper:	**Clay Coat**
Coating:	**Laminate**
Handle Type:	**Soft Cord**

This boutique carries casual clothing and sportswear for men and women. Though *pi* is a Greek letter, when contained within a circle, it symbolizes harmony to the Chinese. The Chinese ideograms which appear to either side of the *pi* mean flair and prestige. The message is reinforced by repetition of the pattern on this elegant bag.

Shopping Bag Title: **State Fair of Texas**
Client: **Texas State Agriculture Commission**
Designer/Art Director: **Mike Hicks**
Firm: **Hixo, Inc., Austin, TX**
Illustrator: **Melissa Grimes**
Manufacturer: **Duro Bag, Ludlow, KY**
Materials
Paper: **White Kraft**
Handle Type: **Twisted Paper**

The State of Texas has a proud agricultural tradition. In recent years, the plight of the small farmer throughout the country has been particularly felt here. In an effort to recall a proud past, and in the hope of fostering a positive approach to the future, the state fair commissioned a bag honoring Texas agriculture. The bag is executed in sepia, black and white, and uses clip-art illustrations to achieve a period feeling. Detailed copy explores Texas' many and varied contributions to American cuisine. The bottom of the bag proudly states, "Made in Texas by Texans."

Shopping Bag Title: **"Don't Bother me, I'm on Vacation!"**
Establishment: **Vacationville U.S.A., Los Angeles, CA**
Designer/Art Director: **Billy Ingram, Los Angeles, CA**
Distributor: **Armor Paper Products Co. Inc., Los Angeles, CA**
Manufacturer: **Tuf-Pac Inc., Ossipee, NH**
Materials
Bag: **Plastic**
Handle Type: **Patch Handle**

Vacationville U.S.A. caters to tourists with a line of more than 500 different T-shirts. The tag line on the back of the bag embodies the store's approach to marketing, "Don't bother me, I'm on vacation." Vicky, the blonde with beachball on the front of the bag further reinforces the theme. The bag is plastic; the feeling, relaxed. It captures the essence of Los Angeles for the visitor.

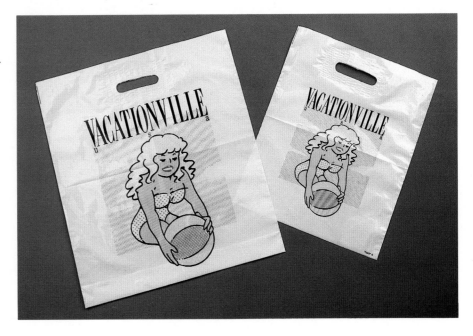

Shopping Bag Title: **Gump's Shopping Bag**
Establishment: **Gump's, San Francisco, CA**
Manufacturer: **Champion International, Walden, NY**
Materials
Paper: **Special Dyed Kraft**
Handle Type: **Black Plastic**

This bag has been used for so long (several decades) that it is difficult to trace who developed it. To afficionados of the store, the distinctive black lettering on the signature red, uncoated stock needs no further explanation. Gump's sells exquisite china, pottery, art, silver and glass from Europe and Asia. Its slogan is, "Where good taste costs no more." The bag need not be intricate nor artful; the name alone serves as a successful marketing device for Gump's.

Shopping Bag Title: **Edison Mall ▶**
Establishment: **Edison Mall, Fort Myers, FL**
Designer/Art Director: **Rex Peteet**
Firm: **Sibley/Peteet Design, Dallas, TX**
Illustrator: **Rex Peteet**
Manufacturer: **Champion International, Walden, NY**
Materials
Paper: **Clay Coat**
Handle Type: **Twisted Paper**

The vibrant image of Thomas Edison, with lightning bolt, reflects the suburban mall's aim to re-establish itself in the marketplace. The bag was conceived as part of a well-coordinated multi-media campaign extolling the mall as a better and more exciting place to shop. The vivid contrast of orange with purple on the white paper bag contributes to the excitement.

Shopping Bag Title:	**Spring Like Never Before**
Establishment:	**Nordstrom, Seattle, WA**
Designer:	**Sydney Hammerquist**
Art Director:	**Cheryl Fujii**
Firm:	**Nordstrom Advertising, Seattle, WA**
Illustrator:	**Tony Kimball**
Calligrapher:	**Bruce Hale**
Manufacturer:	**The Pack Corporation /Osaka, Japan**
Materials Paper:	**Coated**
Coating:	**Laminated**
Handle Type:	**Yellow Acrylic Rope**

The art director was seeking a primitive, perhaps even Mayan, feeling for this bag. The result is not Mayan in the classic sense, but the effect is all the more powerful in that it cannot be precisely defined. The design is fresh; the colors are the light, yet clear, tones associated with spring. One side of the bag features a white face. On the other, the colors are reversed. In many parts of the United States, Spring also has two faces—cold spells alternating with periods of sudden warmth. Perhaps the dichotomy within the season as reflected in the bag is one of the reasons why this bag is among the most popular in the store's history.

Shopping Bag Title:	**Metropolis—The Shape of** ▶ **Things To Come**
Establishment:	**Nordstrom, Seattle, WA**
Designer:	**Kat Thompson**
Art Director:	**Cheryl Fujii**
Firm:	**Nordstrom Advertising, Seattle, WA**
Illustrator:	**Tim Girvin, Seattle, WA**
Printer:	**A.G.I., Chicago, IL**
Manufacturer:	**Champion International, Walden, NY**
Materials	
Paper:	**Clay Coat**
Coating:	**Electron Beam**
Handle Type:	**Blue Plastic**

The contrast of the violet building with two light shades of blue suggests that the store has an innovative approach to marketing. Though the building was intended simply as a generic futuristic image, it is interesting to note that this bag was issued shortly after Nordstrom finalized its plans to renovate an historic building in downtown San Francisco—its first entry into this important market. The architect's plan for the renovation bears a remarkable resemblance to this silhouette.

Shopping Bag Title:	**Basics ($49.00/$17.95 bag)**
Establishment:	**Conran's, New York, NY**
Designer:	**Nicholas Bouyoukas**
Art Director:	**Betty Chow**
Firm:	**Conran's Design Group, New York, NY**
Illustrator:	**Nicholas Bouyoukas**
Manufacturer:	**Champion International, Walden, NY**
Materials	
Paper:	**White Kraft**
Handle Type:	**Twisted Paper**

The Basics bags promote a line of basic, economical home furnishings. To underline the theme, simple shapes are depicted in primary colors. The bags have different but related images on each side so they also form a mural.

Shopping Bag Title: **Summer Inside/Out**
◄ Establishment: **Conran's, New York, NY**
Designer: **Nicholas Bouyoukas**
Art Director: **Betty Chow**
Firm: **Conran's Design Group,**
New York, NY
Illustrator: **Nicholas Bouyoukas**
Manufacturer: **Champion International,**
Walden, NY

Materials
Paper: **White Kraft**
Handle Type: **Kraft**

Faced with a known theme for the
summer line, the designers wanted
an image that was light-hearted and
would translate well into associated
products—windsocks, tee shirts and
fabric banners for use in the store.
The generic fish in the colors planned
for use that season are an appealing
image. The design is loose enough to
work well on flexographic equipment,
and large enough in scale to portray a
striking image on the street.

Shopping Bag Title: **Signature Bag**
Establishment: **Burdines, Miami, FL**
Designer: **Jeanette Bately**
Manufacturer: **Equitable Bag Company,**
Long Island City, NY

Materials
Paper: **Clay Coat**
Handle Type: **Plastic**

This is Burdines' signature bag. The
tropical colors and images of palm
tree and hot sun promote not only the
store, but also the Florida lifestyle. A
series of three bags uses the same bold
graphic. Color combinations vary with
the different bags.

Shopping Bag Title:	**A Matter of Style**	Coating:	**Electron Beam**
Establishment:	**Nordstrom, Seattle, WA**	Handle Type:	**Blue Plastic**
Designer:	**Juli North**		
Art Director:	**Cheryl Fujii**		
Firm:	**Nordstrom Advertising, Seattle, WA**		
Illustrator:	**Brian Bulkley**		
Calligrapher:	**Art Chantry**		
Printer:	**A.G.I., Chicago, IL**		
Manufacturer:	**Champion International, Walden, NY**		
Materials			
Paper:	**Clay Coat**		

An elegant navy blue matte-finish background provides the classic backdrop for stylized hand-lettering in a vivid golden yellow. The contrast of the two colors and the elegance of the letter forms convey—just as the art director intended—the impression of a grand hotel. To ensure that the impression of elegance was complete, a custom-matched plastic handle was specified.

Shopping Bag Title:	**Gift Bag Series: Royale, Reflectif, Potpourri and Magique**
Establishment:	**Germaine Monteil Cosmetiques Corporation, New York, NY**
Designer/Art Director:	**Berett Fisher**
Firm:	**Germaine Monteil, New York, NY**
Photographer:	**Chris Collins**
Distributor:	**Modern Arts Packaging, New York, NY**
Materials	
Paper:	**Clay Coat**
Coating:	**Film Laminate**
Handle Type:	**Soft Loop One Knot**

Germaine Monteil treats its customers to four different gift assortments each year. Using match colors and exquisite photography, each bag clearly shows the particular assortment it will hold. A different colored background is used for each bag, so the customer will be able to determine easily which she already has. The dramatic bags are used in multiples for in-store display, and also pique the interest of passersby on the street. This type of sample giveaway is a proven technique for promoting lesser-known products.

Shopping Bag Title: "Think California"
◄ Establishment: Weinstock's,
Sacramento, CA
Designer: Marianita Howard
Art Director: P. K. Kirtley
Firm: Weinstock's,
Sacramento, CA
Illustrator: Charley Brown
Manufacturer: Duro Bag, Ludlow, KY
Materials
Paper: Clay Coat
Handle Type: Twisted Paper

The image of a golden poppy
superimposed on the ocean accurately
depicts the theme of the promotion
for which it was designed. Weinstock's
had staged a two-week celebration in
honor of California and its incipient
culture. This bag commemorated
an event co-sponsored by the store,
Weinstock's, and the American Express
Company. The vivid colors used on the
bag show up extremely well on the
white clay coat paper.

Shopping Bag Title: **Galleria**
Establishment: **Galleria Shopping
Center/Dallas, Dallas, TX**
Designer/Art Director: **Linda Eissler**
Firm: **Eisenberg Inc., Dallas, TX**
Illustrator: **Mark Drury**
Printer: **A.G.I., Chicago, IL**
Manufacturer: **Champion International,
Walden, NY**
Materials
Paper: **Clay Coat**
Coating: **Electron Beam**
Handle Type: **White Plastic**

The Galleria is a family-oriented
shopping mall that houses various
establishments featuring products from
around the world. The Mall wanted
its shopping bags to emphasize the
multi-national theme in a festive way.
The design solution was achieved
through use of bright colors applied in
quick strokes on a map of the world.
Electron beam coating and white
plastic handles provide a finished look
for the bag.

Shopping Bag Title:	**A Very Special Gift**
Establishment:	**Turtle Creek Partnership, Dallas, TX**
Designers:	**Christina Mann/ Cerita Smith**
Art Directors:	**Christina Mann/ Cerita Smith**
Firm:	**Smith & Mann Design, Dallas, TX**
Illustrator:	**Cerita Smith**
Distributor:	**Turtle Creek Partnership (The invitation bags were all hand-delivered.)**
Manufacturer:	**Various standard items were purchased already produced and modified for the invitation.**

This shopping bag was designed to intrigue the recipient. The tag, ribbons and tissue paper could conceal almost anything. When the bag is opened and the half-gallon ice-cream carton removed, a list of committee members is revealed on one side of the carton and a picture of a tree on the other. Inside the carton is a tiny, living, pine tree. Rolled to fit inside the carton is an invitation to a gala party to raise funds for a new park. The soft pastels of the packaging provide a beautiful backdrop for the star of the show—the living tree.

Shopping Bag Title: **FAO Schwarz**
Establishment: **FAO Schwarz, New York, NY**
Designer: **Claud Langwith**
Distributor: **S. Posner & Sons, New York, NY**
Manufacturer: **Champion International, Walden, NY**
Materials
Paper: **White Kraft**
Handle Type: **Red Plastic**

FAO Schwarz toy store is almost synonymous with wish fulfillment for children. This image is depicted on the bag via rocking horses reversed on block-like backgrounds in bright colors. When the bag is carried, it appears that the horses are actually rocking the blocks back and forth. Bright red plastic handles balance the store's logo at the bottom of the bag in the same shade.

Shopping Bag Title: **To Skipper from the Tail**
Establishment: **Avirex U.S.A.,**
New York, NY
Designer/Art Director: **Mark D. Greenberg**
Firm: **Avirex U.S.A.,**
Long Island City, NY
Materials
Paper: **Clay Coat**
Coating: **Laminate**
Handle Type: **Braided Rope**

The detailed illustration of a World
War II aircraft carrier bomber appears
on both the shopping bag and the hang
tags of this vendor of aviation apparel.
On the other side of the shopping
bag is a photo of a tail gunner, also
taken during World War II. The use of
vintage photography and illustrations
reinforces the company's commitment
to excellence and authenticity in
aviation apparel and equipment.

Shopping Bag Title: **Boundary Waters Bag**
Establishment: **Dayton Hudson Department Store Company, Minneapolis, MN**
Designer: **Patrick Redmond**
Art Director: **Minda Gralnek**
Firm: **Dayton Hudson Department Store Company, Minneapolis, MN**
Illustrator: **Patrick Redmond**
Manufacturer: **Equitable Bag Company, Long Island City, NY**

Materials
Paper: **Kraft**
Handle Type: **White Cord**

"Boundary Waters" is the store's private label. The promotional bag carries out the nautical theme. Before commencing the design process, the artist carefully researched the water-bourne history of the area. Moccasins, various sails and the quintessential dugout grace the bag. Nautical signal flags provide a colorful border along the top of the bag. Immediately below the border are illustrations of sailor's knots.

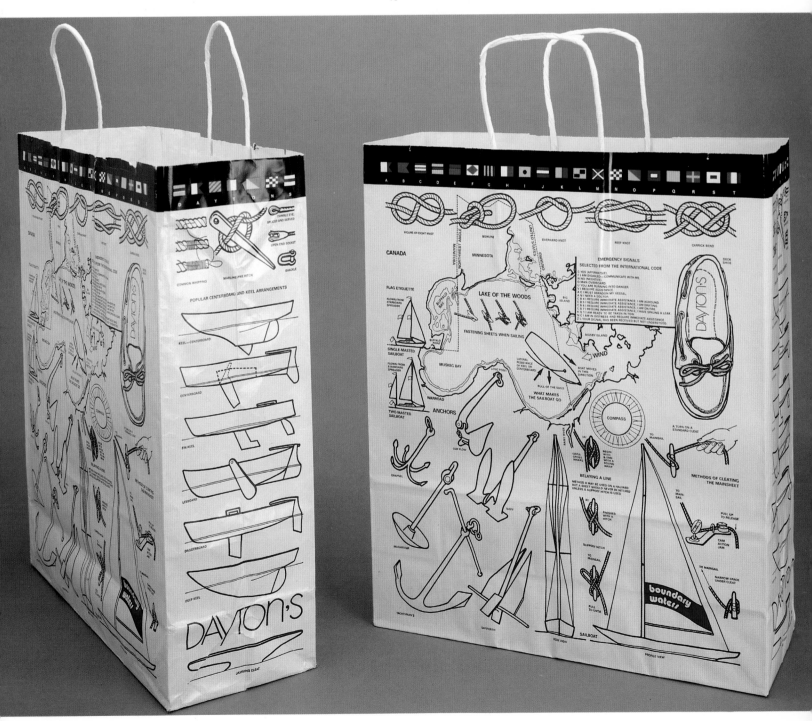

AVIREX LTD.
33-00 47th AVE.
LONG ISLAND CITY N.Y. 11101
TEL; 718-482-1860
FAX; 718-482-1881
TLX; 423016 AVIREX

SHOWROOM
39 WEST 55th STREET
NEW YORK N.Y. 10019 SUITE 302
TEL; 212-245-1465

Shopping Bag Title:	**Flying Flag & Fortress**
Establishment:	**The Cockpit,**
	Long Island City, NY
Designer/Art Director:	**Mark Greenberg**
Firm:	**The Cockpit,**
	Long Island City, NY
Materials	
Paper:	**Clay Coat**
Coating:	**Laminate**
Handle Type:	**Braided Rope**

This boutique specializes in World War II era aviation apparel. The illustration on the shopping bag was originally used for a war bonds poster in 1942, and amply reflects the romance of early aviation. Nostalgia, pride in America and the joyous sensation of "taking off" are captured in the illustration. The same artwork is used on the cover of The Cockpit's mail order catalog.

Shopping Bag Art

CHAPTER

9

Most shopping bags promote an establishment's corporate identity or advertise a very special event. Occasionally, they "rise above themselves" and become a unique artistic statement. These rare instances of the creation of beauty, almost for its own sake, is celebrated in this chapter.

All the shopping bags included here are examples not only of great design, but also of exquisite printing and finishing techniques. A beautiful shopping bag, like any other reproduced piece, is a masterpiece created by many hands.

Shopping Bag Title:	**Modern Impressions**
Establishment:	**Nordstrom, Seattle, WA**
Designer:	**Juli North**
Art Director:	**Cheryl Fujii**
Firm:	**Nordstrom Advertising, Seattle, WA**
Illustrator/Calligrapher:	**Anton C. Kimball**
Manufacturer:	**Champion International, Walden, NY**
Printer:	**A.G.I.**
Materials	
Paper:	**Clay Coat**
Handle:	**Twisted Paper**
Coating:	**Electron Beam**

Monet's studies of water lilies at Giverny were the inspiration for these bags, but *modern* impressions are the theme behind the design. Consequently, one side of the bag is impressionist in feeling; the other is post-impressionist, reminiscent of Rousseau. Other bags in the series also connect Monet's art with the modern era.

Shopping Bag Title:	Simply Sensational!
Establishment:	Broadway Southwest, Mesa, AZ
Designer/Art Director:	Walter Herrington
Firm:	Herrington & Soter, Inc., Los Angeles, CA
Illustrator:	Mark Dickson
Distributor:	The Reuben Schneider Company, Phoenix, AZ
Manufacturer:	The Pack Corporation, Osaka, Japan
Materials	
Paper:	Clay Coated
Coating:	Laminate
Handle Type:	Soft Cord
Special Finishing:	5-color Process
Special Name:	Tags Hand-Affixed to handles

"Simply Sensational!" was the theme chosen by the store to celebrate the opening of its first two outlets in the Denver area. The bag was a gift to customers on opening day. To enhance the perceived value of the bag, the store is identified only by a tag attached to the purple polypropylene handle. To position the bag as uniquely Coloradan, a local artist's work was chosen for the illustration.

Shopping Bag Title:	**Homage to Matisse**
Designer:	**George Corsillo**
Art Director:	**Elaine Cumiskey**
Firm:	**The Stephen Lawrence Company, Carlstadt, NJ**
Distributor:	**The Stephen Lawrence Company, Carlstadt, NJ**
Materials	
Paper:	**Clay Coat**
Coating:	**Plastic Laminate**
Handle Type:	**Pink Cotton Cord**

One of the newest trends in shopping bag design is the gift bag—that is, a bag which is designed to be used with color-coordinated tissue paper in lieu of gift wrapping. This Euro-style bag, in homage to Matisse, is accented with hand-finished pink cotton cord handles.

Shopping Bag Title:	**Renoir**	One of the paintings from the museum's travelling exhibit was reproduced on the shopping bag which advertises the exhibit's scheduled display in Boston. The bag is both a memento of one's visit to the museum and a means of transporting other purchases from the gift shop. The sale of such a bag is one means of financing the exhibit. Other possibilities involving shopping bags include a coop arrangement with a corporate sponsor whose name might appear in the gusset.
Establishment:	**Museum of Fine Arts, Boston, MA**	
Concept:	**Spencer O'Loughlin and Rae Wakelin of PAK 2000**	
Production/Logo design:	**Carl Zahn, Museum of Fine Arts, Boston**	
Illustrator:	**Renoir**	
Manufacturer:	**PAK 2000, Mirror Lake, NH**	
Materials		
Paper:	**Coated**	
Handle Type:	**Soft Cord**	

Shopping Bag Title:	**John Singer Sargent Gift Bag**
Establishment:	**Art Institute of Chicago, Chicago, IL**
Designer:	**Ann Wassmann Gross**
Firm:	**Art Institute of Chicago, Chicago, IL**
Illustrator:	**John Singer Sargent**
Manufacturer:	**PAK 2000, Mirror Lake, NH**
Materials	
Paper:	**Coated**
Coating:	**Laminate**
Handle Type:	**Soft Cord**
Special Finishing:	**Offset Litho**

This bag was one of several items sold in connection with an exhibit of Sargent's work. As "advertising" for the subject matter and for the exhibit, it works very well. The cord handles have been chosen carefully to harmonize with the colors in the illustration. Information about the exhibit appears only in the gussets.

Shopping Bag Title:	"The Cockpit Wins Again"
Establishment:	Cockpit U.S.A., New York, NY
Designers:	Jeff Clyman/Jackie Clyman
Art Directors:	Frank Marchese/ Marty Wolk, Long Island City, NY
Manufacturer:	Intergraphitalia, Italy
Materials	
Paper:	Coated
Coating:	Laminate
Handle Type:	Soft Cord

Semi-realistic poster art typical of the World War II era was used for this bag. The romance, glamour and fearful excitement inherent in early aviation is captured in the design. The glossy laminate finish enhances the poster effect. Black rope handles provide a discreet means of carrying the Euro-style bag without detracting the poster effect.

Shopping Bag Title:	Eiko Ishioka Shopping Bag
Establishment:	Dayton Hudson Department Store Company, Minneapolis, MN
Designer:	Eiko Ishioka
Art Director:	Eiko Ishioka
Firm:	Dayton Hudson Department Store Company, Minneapolis, MN
Photographer:	Bishin Jumonji
Manufacturer:	Champion International, Walden, NY
Printer:	A.G.I.
Materials	
Paper:	Clay Coat
Coating:	Electron Beam
Handle Type:	Pink Tinted Twisted Paper

This bag was commissioned in celebration of not one, but two special events: Bachman's Flower Show and the Walker Art Center's "Tokyo: Form and Spirit" exhibition. Because of time considerations, an existing illustration by one of the illustrators featured in the art exhibit was selected for the bag. The mechanicals and copy were sent to her in Tokyo. A few weeks later, she had transformed these into a bag with which the store was delighted. Among designer Ishioka's recent projects was the design of the setting for the successful Aid & Comfort benefit of the San Francisco-based Aids Foundation held in June 1987.

Shopping Bag Title:	**David Hockney Shopping Bag**	Commissioned for the British Festival of Minnesota, sponsored by the Walker Art Center, this bag depicts a pair of characters dear to the hearts of all British children—the puppets, Punch and Judy. To underline the point, the British flag appears above Punch and Judy's stage. The gussets, which use the colors of the British flag, tell the story of the Festival.
Establishment:	**Dayton Hudson Department Store Company, Minneapolis, MN**	
Designer:	**Robert Valentine**	
Art Director:	**Minda Gralnek**	
Firm:	**Dayton Hudson Department Store Company, Minneapolis, MN**	
Illustrator:	**David Hockney**	
Manufacturer:	**Champion International, Walden, NY**	
Printing:	**A.G.I.**	
Materials		
Paper:	**White Kraft**	
Coating:	**Electron Beam**	
Handle Type:	**Black Plastic**	

Shopping Bag Title:	**Homage to Monet**
Designer:	**George Corsillo**
Art Director:	**Elaine Cumiskey**
Firm:	**The Stephen Lawrence Co., Carlstadt, NJ**
Distributor:	**The Stephen Lawrence Company, Carlstadt, NJ**
Materials	
Paper:	**Printed Offset**
Coating:	**Plastic Laminate**
Handle Type:	**Purple Cotton Cord**

This gift bag uses Monet's familiar water lilies and reproduces the clear light colors from his garden at Giverny to evoke a soft, artistic feeling. The luminous colors are further enhanced by plastic laminate coating.

Shopping Bag Title: **Cloud-Bag**
Establishment: **E. G. Smith Inc.,**
New York, NY
Designer/Art Director: **Seth Jaben**
Firm: **Seth Jaben Studio,**
New York, NY
Illustrator/Photographer: **Seth Jaben**
Distributor: **Modern Arts Packaging,**
New York, NY
Materials
Paper: **Clay Coat**
Coating: **Laminate**
Handle Type: **Soft Cord**

Four different cloud bags, when placed
next to each other, form a continuous
mural. The wit and whimsy of the bags
is a reflection of the company's attitude
towards its product—gaily colored
socks—and its spirited customers.
The bags are provided as a gift with
the purchase of three pairs of socks.
The artist, whose philosophy is "Art is
Advertising," chose clouds for the bag
so that city dwellers could possess a
little piece of sky, even if they had to
carry it with them.

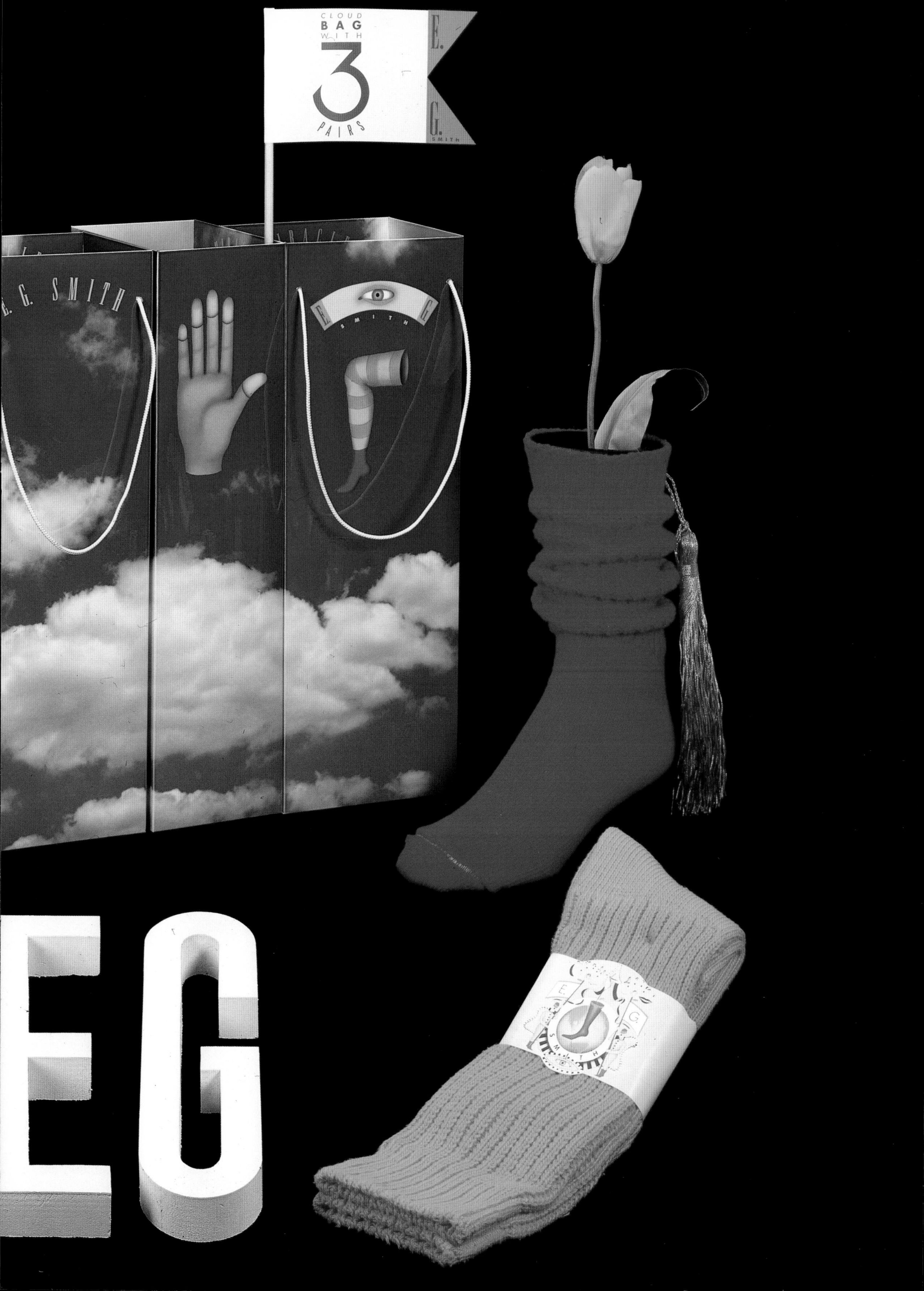
CLOUD
BAG
WITH
3
PAIRS
E.
G.
SMITH
E. G. SMITH
EG

Picasso

Shopping Bag Title:	Tete De Femme
Establishment:	Marigold Enterprises, Ltd., New York, NY
Art Director:	Marilyn R. Goldberg
Firm:	Marigold Enterprises, Ltd., New York, NY
Photographer:	Transparency taken from Pablo Picasso's estate
Artist:	Pablo Picasso
Manufacturer:	EL PAC, LTD., Monroe, NY
Materials	
Paper:	Coated
Coating:	Laminate
Handle Type:	Soft Cord

Marigold produces a variety of lines such as fine greeting cards, shopping bags, and playing cards. The products feature the work of noted artists and are marketed strictly through museums and art galleries. These beautiful reproductions of the work of Pablo Picasso on Euro-style bags are typical of Marigold's products.

Shopping Bag Title:	**Hollywood Legend & Reality**
Establishment:	**Smithsonian Institution Travelling Exhibition, Washington, D.C.**
Designer:	**Doug Johnson, New York, NY**
Illustrator:	**Doug Johnson**
Manufacturer:	**PAK 2000,**
Distributed by:	**S.I.T.E.**
Materials	
Paper:	**Coated**
Coating:	**Laminate**
Handle Type:	**Soft Cord**
Special Finishing:	**Offset Litho**

Designed to coordinate with a travelling exhibit, this Art Deco bag brilliantly evokes the glamour of Hollywood's hey-day in the 1930's. Soft pastels, sleek automobiles and the suggestion of searchlights convey the idea of a star-studded premiere. The focial point of this glossy bag is a half-glimpsed screen kiss. Who are the actors? Gable, Dietrich, Grant? It is left to the observer's imagination, For, after all, the charm of Hollywood is make-believe.

Shopping Bag Title: **Floral Collection**
Establishment: **The Gifted Line,**
John Grossman, Inc.,
Sausalito, CA

Designer/Art Director:

John Grossman
Firm: **The Gifted Line,**
John Grossman, Inc.
Photographer: **Jon Wells**
Manufacturer: **Artpack, New York, NY**
Materials
Paper: **Coated**
Coating: **Laminated**
Handle Type: **Gold Soft Cord**
Special Finishing: **Hand Assembled**

Using images drawn from late 19th/ early 20th century art, John Grossman, Inc. has developed a broad variety of gift packaging. The bags range in size from a two-inch cube box to a full size shopping tote and provide a way to package anything. Also available are sheets of wrapping paper with the same pattern and coordinated gift tags. Because the bags are designed for reuse, their construction is exceptionally sturdy, with tag-stock bottom inserts and reinforcements for the lip. A high-gloss heavy laminate finish protects the outside of the bag. Hand-affixed cord handles in a coordinated color provide an elegant finishing touch. This particular design was drawn from an album of various die-cut scraps assembled in 1895 by Emma Johnson. Other lines available include a Christmas series, and flower fantasies, both drawn primarily from Victorian postcards.

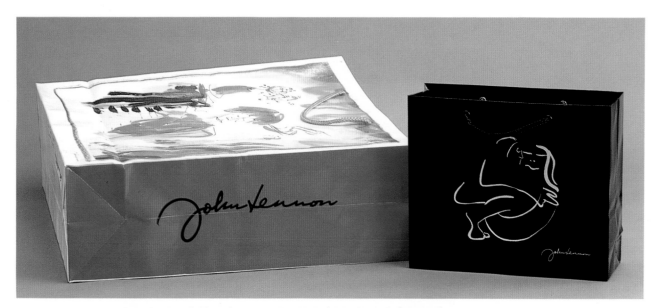

Shopping Bag Title:	"Bag One" and "Grand Piano" Gift Bags
Establishment:	Marigold Enterprises Ltd., New York, NY
Art Director:	Marilyn R. Goldberg
Firm:	Marigold Enterprises Ltd., New York, NY
Illustrator:	John Lennon
Manufacturer:	PAK 2000, Mirror Lake, NH Distributed to Museums and Galleries by Marigold Enterprises, Ltd.
Materials	
Paper:	Coated
Coating:	Laminate
Handle Type:	Soft Cord

Designer bags are now frequently illustrated by famous artists. Usually, however, the artist prepares a design specifically for a shopping bag. These line drawings are by a very famous artist, indeed—John Lennon. Lennon's original drawings have been reproduced on highly laminated Euro-style bags. "Grand Piano" was, like "Bag One," originally a simple line drawing. Color was added to the original line drawing in "Grand Piano."

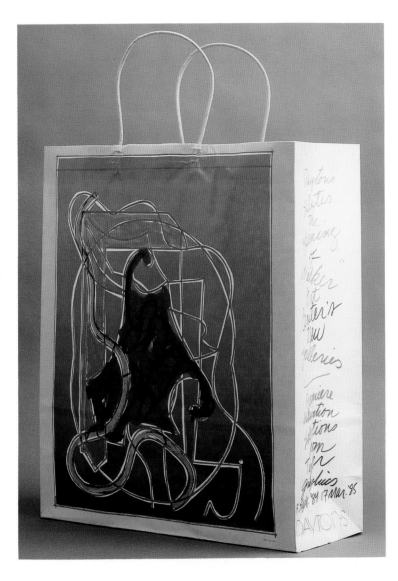

Shopping Bag Title:	**Frank Stella Shopping Bag**
Establishment:	**Dayton Hudson Department Store Company, Minneapolis, MN**
Designer:	**Karen Brown**
Art Director:	**Minda Gralnek**
Firm:	**Dayton Hudson Department Store Company, Minneapolis, MN**
Illustrator:	**Frank Stella**
Manufacturer:	**Champion International, Walden, NY**
Printer:	**A.G.I.**
Materials	
Paper:	**White Kraft**
Coating:	**Electron Beam**
Handle Type:	**Tinted Twisted Paper**

This bag was commissioned as a salute to the opening of the Walker Art Center, and features the artwork of an illustrator whose work was exhibited there. The designer used colors drawn from the illustration to explain the bag's story, via the copy in the gussets. A matte, rather than glossy, finish was selected to enhance the illustrator's art.

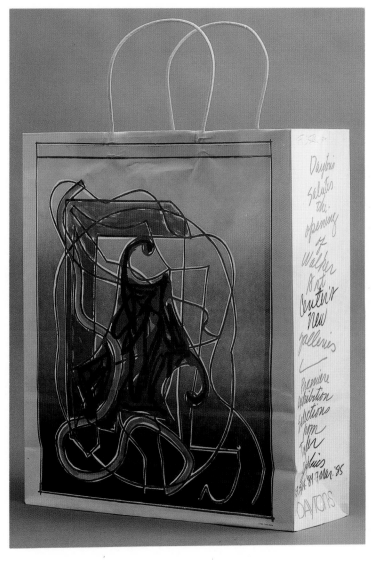

Icons of Popular Culture

CHAPTER

10

Shopping bags are so much a part of our lifestyle that they have moved beyond their original arena to assume new and unusual forms. Shopping bags now appear as invitations, prospectuses, vases and pots for houseplants. In at least one instance, they have been used as in-store signage for a large grocery store! The reverse side of this coin is *trompe l'oeil* bags which imitate other objects. Bags can look like briefcases, the objects they are designed to carry (shirts and ties, for example), or a woman's handbag.

In both instances of life imitating art and art imitating life, the lines between reality and fantasy blur. Shopping bags have finally provided an ironic retort to the tongue-in-cheek use Warhol and Lichtenstein made of them—they have become icons of *our* popular culture.

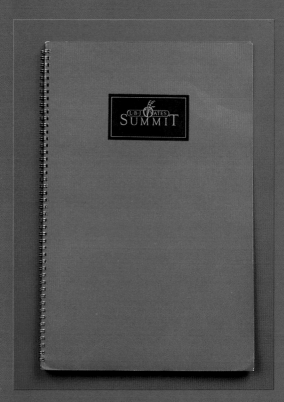

Shopping Bag Title: **Brochure**
Establishment: **LBJ Oates/Summit**
Dallas, TX
Designer: **Michael Krackenberger**
Creative Director: **Steve Connatser**
Firm: **Connatser & Company,**
Dallas, TX

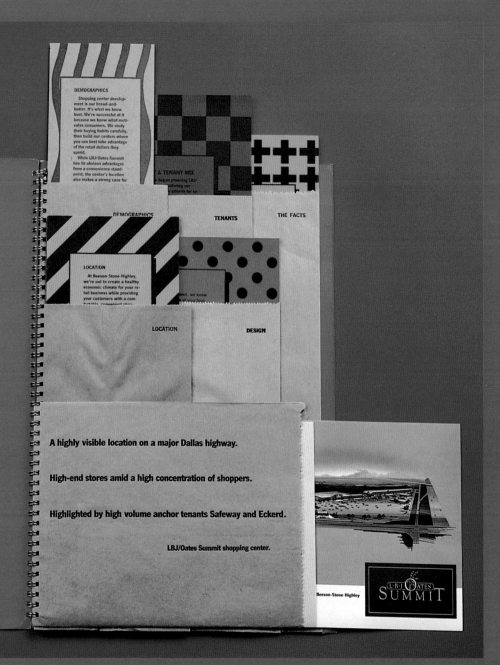

How better to present the prospectus for a new shopping center than with shopping bags? Vividly colored cards peek out from standard brown bags which are affixed in a cherry red cardboard, spiral bound cover. Flexographic typography identifies the specific areas of interest covered by the cards in each bag. This format makes excellent use of a technique most frequently employed in direct mail solicitations. Known in the trade as an "involvement device," it forces the recipient to actively take part in disassembling the packaging in order to obtain information.

Shopping Bag Title:	"Flight No. 1712, Only Nuts Fly 2nd Class"
Establishment:	**Bag Advertising, Inc., Denver, CO**
Designer:	**Vicki Gullickson**
Art Director:	**Errol Beauchamp**
Firm:	**Bag Advertising, Inc., Denver, CO**
Illustrator:	**Vicki Gullickson**
Materials	
Paper:	**Kraft**
Special Finishing:	**Four-color offset Invitation Inside Bag**

Using pre-made Kraft bags as carriers, this graphic arts company cleverly incorporated its modus operandi into an invitation to an open house. The contrast between the brown bag, which was actually mailed, and the colorful invitation, is a nice blend of the prosaic and the entertaining. Because a bag is an unusual item to receive in the mail, it also ensured the recipient would look at what was inside.

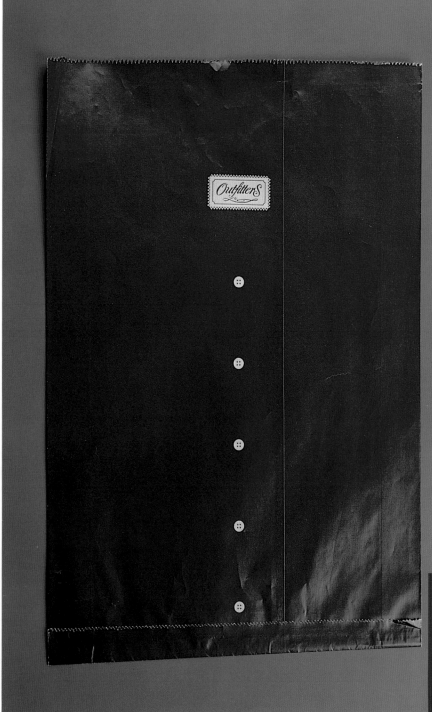

Shopping Bag Title: **Outfitters Shirt Bag**
Establishment: **Outfitters, Dallas, TX**
Designer: **Carol Burke**
Art Director: **Cap Pannell/Carol Burke**
Firm: **Pannel/St. George,
Dallas, TX**
Illustrator: **Carol Burke**
Distributor: **G Sales, Garland, TX**
Manufacturer: **St. Clair Pakwell,
Wilsonville, OR**

Material
Paper: **Clay Coated**

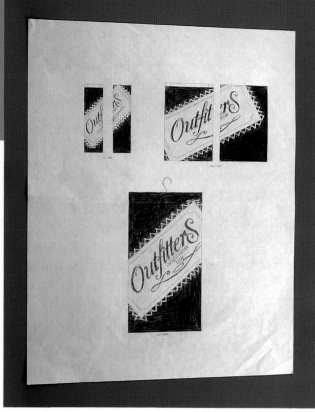

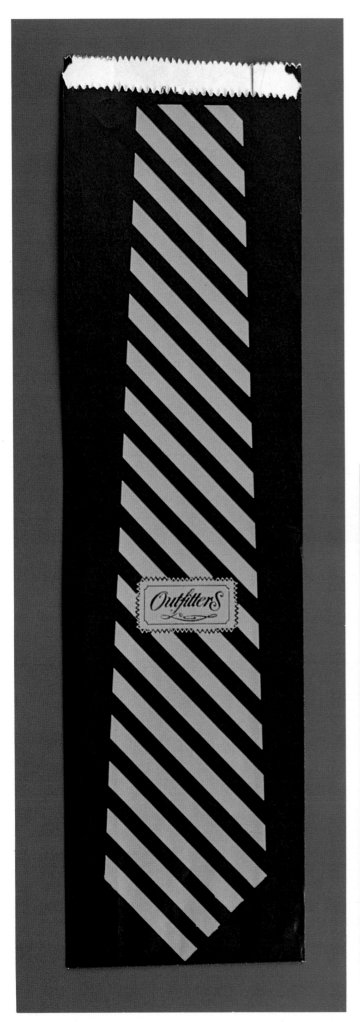

Buttons march down the front of this bag designed just for shirts. There is no chance the shopper will confuse the bagged shirt with its accompanying bagged tie. Size and shape are not the only differences. A regimental tie adorns the tie bag; the store name appears as a discreet tie tac. The deep green and cream color scheme lends a dignified air to the slightly humorous design. Shopping is not, after all, a serious activity—except to the retailer!

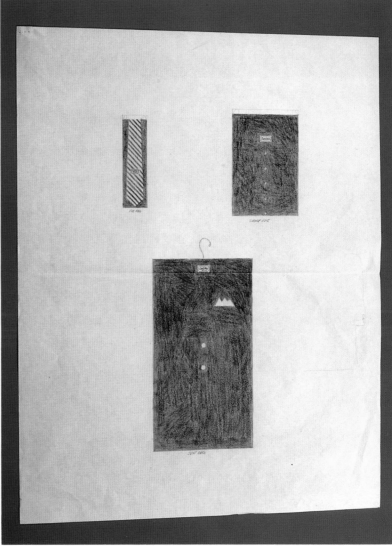

Promotional Item: **This Christmas more than 250,000 shoppers are in the bag . . .**

Establishment: **Southwest Media Corp. (D MAGAZINE). Dallas, TX**

Designer: **Cerita Smith**

Art Director: **Cerita Smith/Cap Pannell**

Firm: **Cap Pannel & Company, Dallas, TX**

Materials Manufacture: **6¼″ × 10″ white sacks were purchased and printed labels were applied to the outside of the sacks and also used to close the blue tissue wrapped around the promotion piece.**

This direct mail promotional piece is a visual pun on a familiar adage. Bags have become so much a part of our culture that they are a recognizable factor in the American vernacular. The packaging theme is continued through the various pieces, which promote a special Christmas issue, culminating in a window on each brochure panel which finally becomes a Christmas package. Imaginatively designed labels provide a cost-effective means to transform ordinary white bags and blue tissue paper into a very personal package.

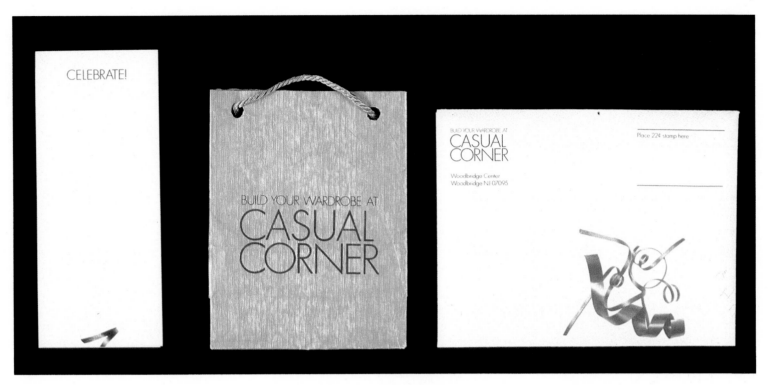

Shopping Bag Title:	**Invitation Bag, Build Your Wardrobe At . . .**
Establishment:	**Casual Corner, Enfield, CT**
Designer:	**Scott Bolestridge**
Art Director:	**Robert P. Gersin**
Firm:	**Robert P. Gersin Assoc., Inc., New York, NY**
Distributor:	**Party Bazaar, New York, NY**
Materials Paper:	**Silver Foil**
Handle Type:	**Twisted Paper**

When a new store opened, with a new interior design and revised marketing approach, Casual Corner announced the event with an invitation enclosed in a miniature shopping bag. To reinforce the message of the new look and approach, the chain's logo and color palette were also changed. The new look of the invitation bag successfully points up a new look for the store.

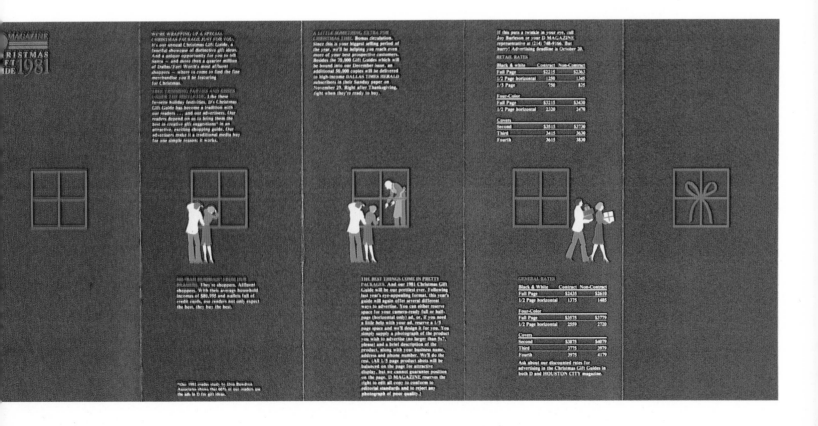

This purveyor of paper products used an ordinary brown Kraft bag as the envelope for its die-cut, two-color Grand Opening announcement. Custom labels seal the bag and lend a note of excitement to this direct mail piece. Until the recipient actually reads the announcement copy, he cannot be sure of the nature of the establishment—is this take-out food or paper supply?

Shopping Bag Title:	**Dixon Take Out**
Establishment:	**Dixon Paper Center, Denver, CO**
Designer:	**Martin Miller**
Art Director:	**Errol Beauchamp**
Firm:	**The Beauchamp Group, Inc., Denver, CO**
Illustrator:	**Martin Miller**
Distributor:	**Kistler Communications, Denver, CO**
Materials	
Paper:	**Kraft Pint Liquor Bag**
Coating:	**One-color Label**
Special Finishing:	**Two-color Offset Printing on Diecut Sandwich Announcement**

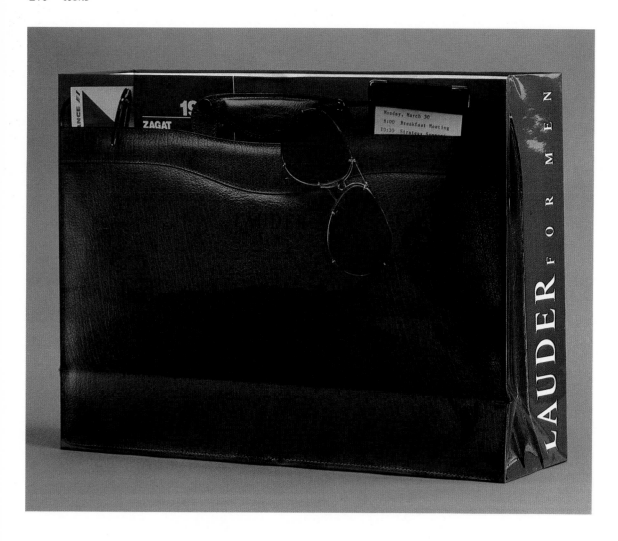

Shopping Bag Title:	**Estee Lauder**
Establishment:	**Estee Lauder Men,** **New York, NY**
Designers:	**Karrie Lane and** **Deborah Leeds**
Firm:	**Estee Lauder,** **New York, NY**
Distributor:	**PAK 2000,** **Mirror Lake, NH**
Materials	
Paper:	**Coated**
Coating:	**Laminate**
Special Finishing:	**Offset Litho**
Handle Type:	**Soft Cord**

These duotone bags are designed to look like a briefcase. In marked contrast to the more typical, feminine-styled designer bags, these achieve a masculine feeling with images of a calculator, pocket atlas and decidedly masculine sunglasses peeping from the "top" of the briefcase's outer pockets. High-quality photographic reproduction and a high-gloss varnish, along with a hand-affixed soft cord handle secured by grommets, lend notes of elegance.

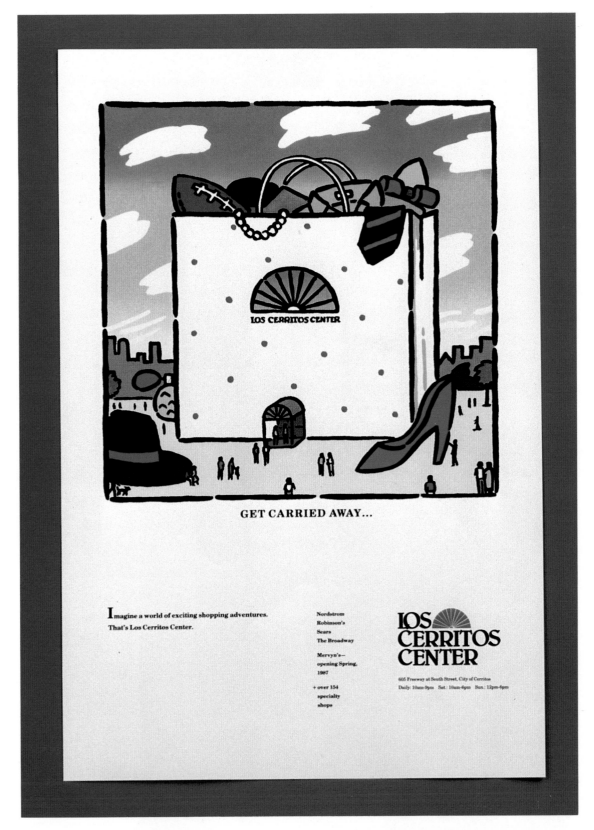

GET CARRIED AWAY...

Imagine a world of exciting shopping adventures.
That's Los Cerritos Center.

Nordstrom
Robinson's
Sears
The Broadway

Mervyn's—
opening Spring,
1987

+ over 154
specialty
shops

LOS CERRITOS CENTER

605 Freeway at South Street, City of Cerritos
Daily: 10am-9pm Sat: 10am-6pm Sun: 12pm-6pm

Shopping Bag Title:	**Get Carried Away**
Establishment:	**Los Cerritos Center, Cerritos, CA**
Designers:	**John Coy, Laurie Handler**
Art Director:	**John Coy**
Firm:	**Coy, Los Angeles, Culver City, CA**
Illustrator:	**Scott Baldwin**

The giant shopping bag as store in this print ad evolved from a campaign involving ordinary objects which had become disproportionately large. The shopping bag is particularly interesting because of the bag's role as a mobile extension of the store. The visual paradox of store-as-bag, bag-as-store injects a pleasing note of whimsy into the ad. The cartooning reminds us that shopping *can* be a realization of fantasy.

Poster Title: **Paper is Our Bag**
Establishment: **Paper Parlour Ltd.,**
Portland, OR
Designer: **Ann Marra**
Firm: **Marra & Associates Graphic**
Design, Portland, OR

This purveyor of quality papers used a folded, lightweight version of this shopping bag poster as a direct mail piece. If the recipient came into the store, he or she could ask for and obtain the unfolded poster on heavier stock. The poster was designed to be a traffic-building device as part of a coordinated three-year direct mail campaign. The shopping bag is both a play on words and a powerful visual statement for the store.

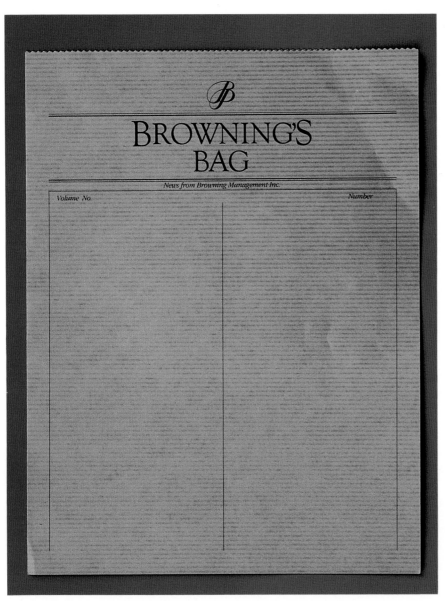

Shopping Bag Title:	Browning's Bag
Establishment:	Browning Management, Dallas, TX
Designer:	Cerita Smith
Art Director:	Cerita Smith
Firm:	Cerita Smith Design, Dallas, TX
Illustrator:	Cerita Smith
Materials Manufacture:	Newsletter shells printed one color blue and die cut pink top.
Stock:	Carnival groove khaki

This internal newsletter for a property management company plays on the company name, Browning's, and the modern slang phrase "What's your bag?" To lend verisimilitude to the bag look, the top edge of the newsletter is die-cut to resemble a bag. The light-heartedness, warmth and informality of the design encourage company employees to explore the newsletter's contents.

Shopping Bag Title:	The Brown Bag Porch Sitting and Dirty Talk Society
Establishment:	Irving Werbin Associates, Mamaroneck, NY
Designer:	Irv Werbin
Art Director:	Irv Werbin
Firm:	Werbin Associates, Mamaroneck, NY
Illustrator:	Irv Werbin
Manufacturer:	Union Camp
Material Paper:	Brown Kraft

This invitation to a social gathering is just plain fun. The extremely formal typeface provides a delightful contrast to the inviting rockers. Placing the invitation on a plain brown grocery bag heightens the humor. The matte white ink used for the rockers creates a strong visual image and a focal point for the design.

Shopping Bag Title:	**Doggie Bag**
Establishment:	**The Gifted Line,**
	John Grossman Inc.,
	Sausalito, CA
Designer:	**John Grossman**
Firm:	**The Gifted Line,**
	John Grossman Inc.,
	Sausalito, CA
Distributor:	**The Gifted Line,**
	Sausalito, CA
Printer:	**A.G.I., Chicago, IL**
Materials	
Paper:	**Clay Coat**
Coating:	**Laminate**

A "doggie bag" is so much a part of American culture that there are generic doggie bags. In a humorous twist on this theme, here is a "doggie bag" that is a gift bag. In homage to the original purpose, the "doggies" are in formal wear at a formal dinner party. The accoutrements in the overall scene, the formal wear of the animals, and the illustration style are 19th century in feeling. The effect is a certain spurious dignity—which enhances the richness of the joke.

Shopping Bag Title:	**Peace**	The white dove floats against a serene
Establishment:	**Brian Collentine Design,**	blue and green background on this
	Los Angeles, CA	art studio's Christmas promotional
Designer/Art Director:	**Brian Collentine**	mailing. The images are paper-stenciled
Firm:	**Brian Collentine Design,**	onto generic white shopping bags,
	Los Angeles, CA	and present a vivid and personalized
Manufacturer:	**Duro Bag, Ludlow, KY**	Christmas message to the store's
Materials		clientele. When is a bag not a bag?
Paper:	**White Kraft**	When it is mailed, folded flat, as a
Handle Type:	**Twisted Paper**	"postcard"—just as this one was.
Special Finishing:	**Screen Printed**	

Promotion Title:	Oakwell Farms Signage
Client:	Oakwell Farms Retail Center, San Antonio, TX
Designers/Art Directors:	Bradford Lawton and Roger Christian
Firm:	Roger Christian & Company, Inc., San Antonio, TX
Sign Manufacturer:	Pro Signs, San Antonio, TX

Oakwell Farms is a planned development which will include a mix of retail establishments. Bored with billboards featuring renderings of retail centers and the numbers to call for information, the developer asked for a sign that would visually pique interest. The design solution was this immense shopping bag at the site of the retail center. The residential section of the development is now complete. The retail portion is under construction. The shopping bag will be retained and, as space is leased, be "filled" with the items featured at the various stores. Examples might include a tie to symbolize menswear, or a book for a bookstore. Apart from its charm as an icon, this sign is a fine example of planning ahead—though designed for use during construction, it will remain applicable when the center is in full operation.

Shopping Bag Title:	**Basics**
Establishment:	**Conran's, New York, NY**
Designer:	**Kristin Johnson/**
	Helen Lepaw
Art Director:	**Kristin Johnson,**
	New York, NY
Illustrator:	**Kristin Johnson**
Manufacturer:	**Champion International,**
	Walden, NY
Materials	
Paper:	**White Kraft**
Handle Type:	**Twisted Paper**

Conran's produces a line of simple, inexpensive furnishings called "Basics." The shopping bag reinforces this theme through simple lines and basic colors. The bag design evolved as the two designers experimented with cut-out images in various assemblages until the whimsical final design was achieved. The necktie draped casually over the top drawer of the bureau is fun, as is the fork spearing the letter "A" on the opposite side. The string handle is, indeed, very basic.

New Frontiers

CHAPTER

11

New Frontiers

The shopping bag started as a practical, unassuming paper object designed for one-time usage. It has progressed in many directions since. After examining its past and present, it seems logical to explore possibilities for the future.

Possible trends are: three-dimensional effects incorporated onto flat surfaces; the use of new materials, more sophisticated manufacturing techniques, unusual handle types and configurations; and the effects of the application of computer technology to shopping bag design. No holograms have appeared as yet, but with the recent advent of their use on credit cards, can their appearance on shopping bags be far behind? After all, the two are symbiotically linked.

A few designers are already forecasting trends for the future in their present work. Examples of these forays in this "new frontier" are featured here.

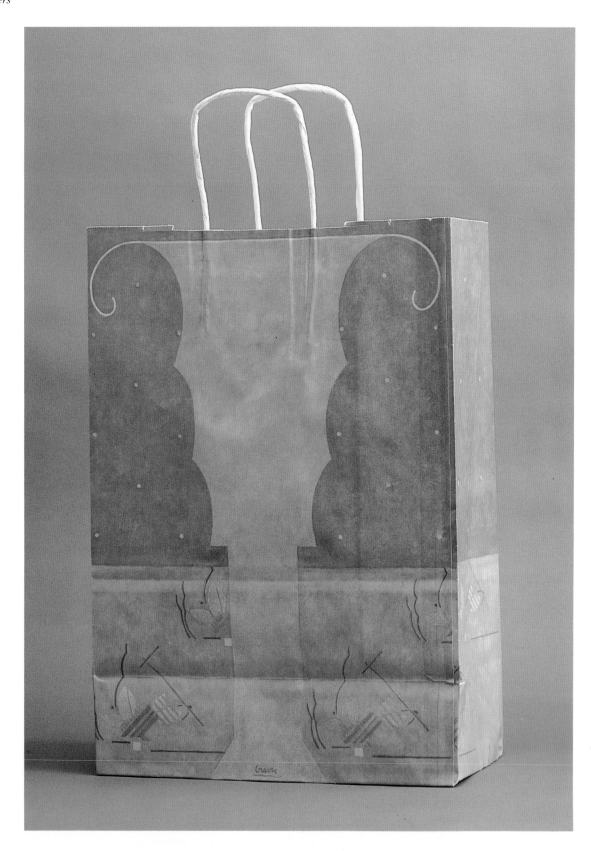

Shopping Bag Title:	**Michael Graves Bag**	
Establishment:	**Bloomingdale's,**	
	New York, NY	
Designer/Illustrator:	**Michael Graves**	
Creative Director:	**John Jay**	
Firm:	**Bloomingdale's,**	
	New York, NY	
Manufacturer:	**Equitable Bag Company,**	
	Long Island City, NY	
Materials		
Paper:	**Clay Coat**	
Handle Type:	**Twisted Paper**	

Graves, a noted architect, used a classic urn as the focus for this bag. The symmetrical form is depicted in the soft shades associated with spring but without the gardens, flowers, and greenery generally used to depict the visual image of spring. Because of the restraint of the design, the message is subtle and elegant. Michael Graves was selected as the designer because he helped the client change views on color. Also, so many people were interpreting his work, the client decided they wanted the original!

Shopping Bag Title:	**Maison Gastronome Ltd.**
Establishment:	**Maison Gastronome, Plandome, NY**
Designer:	**Mindy Waters**
Firm:	**Modern Arts Packaging, New York, NY**
Distributor:	**Modern Arts Packaging, New York, NY**
Materials	
Paper:	**Coated**
Coating:	**Laminate**
Handle Type:	**Soft Cord**
Special Finishing:	**Die Cut with Acetate and Sparkles**

This store specializes in hand-crafted crystal. The way in which the store's image is represented via the bag reflects an advance in shopping bag design. A three-dimensional acrylic insert fits a die-cut on the laminated bag and is partially filled with sparkles. When the bag moves the sparkles shift, suggesting the bubbles in champagne. Black, soft cord provides elegant handles for the bag.

Shopping Bag Title:	**Fresh Air Fare**
Establishment:	**Continental Airlines, Houston, TX**
Designer:	**Miller, Judson, Ford, Houston, TX**
Firm:	**Scali, McCabe & Sloves, New York, NY**
Manufacturer:	**Champion International, Walden, NY**
Materials	
Paper:	**Clay Coat**
Handle Type:	**Twisted Paper**
Special Finishing:	**Flexography**

These refreshing pastel mini-bags are used by the airline to serve in-flight snacks. The bag's message is spelled out in clear copy on one face of the bag. The snacks provided are light and wholesome—fresh fruit, salads and the like. The underlying message—that eating lightly reduces the chance of "traveler's tummy"—is suggested, but never specifically stated. This is an unusual departure for the airline industry and marks the opening of a fresh market for shopping bags.

Shopping Bag Title:	**Fête des Fleurs**
Establishment:	**Neiman-Marcus, Carrollton, TX**
Designer:	**Michael Matthews**
Firm:	**Neiman-Marcus, Dallas, TX**
Manufacturer:	**Champion International, Walden, NY**
Printer:	**A.G.I. Chicago, IL**
Materials	
Paper:	**Clay Coat**
Coating:	**Electron Beam**
Handle Type:	**Soft Cord**

Traditionally, cosmetics vendors use their own bags to promote new products. This bag is a rare cooperative effort among several different companies. Neiman-Marcus arranged the entire promotion. The bag is exciting, not only for the beauty of its design, but also because the handles mark a major step forward. This type of handle is usually affixed by hand. By stiffening the handle ends with plastic, the manufacturer was able to reduce significantly the amount of hand work, thus reducing the overall cost per bag.

Shopping Bag Title:	**Henry Lehr**
Establishment:	**Henry Lehr, New York, NY**
Designer/Art Director:	**John De Stefano**
Firm:	**Modern Arts Packaging, New York, NY**
Distributor:	**Modern Arts Packaging, New York, NY**
Materials	
Paper:	**White Kraft**
Special Finishing:	**Heat Stamp Imprint**
Handle Type:	**Silver/Grey Rigid Plastic**

This unusual bag is part of a coordinated program which includes stationery, signage and three different sizes of bags. Its simplicity is somewhat misleading. In creating the program, the designer took full advantage of recent technological advances. The logotype was output from a MacIntosh computer and associated laser printer. The letters are heat stamped, embossed in red on a deep grey background and printed on white Kraft paper.

Shopping Bag Title:	**Back of Beyond**
Establishment:	**Donaldson's,**
	Minneapolis, MN
Designer:	**Sharon Werner**
Art Director:	**Joe Duffy**
Firm:	**Duffy Design Group,**
	Minneapolis, MN
Illustrator:	**Joe Duffy**
Manufacturer:	**Rainbow Signs/Haileys Mill,**
	Minneapolis, MN
Materials	
Paper:	**Kraft Paper**
Special Finishing:	**Hand Assembled**
Handle Type:	**Flat Kraft**

"Back of Beyond" was an in-store promotion highlighting Australia and the South Pacific. The design combined native artistic motifs, native animals and stickers to highlight the travel theme. Coordinated boxes and point-of-purchase display posters were keyed to the theme bag. The travel theme is underlined by the shape of the bag—horizontal rather than vertical rectangular construction—and by the hand-affixed luggage-type handle.

Shopping Bag Title: **New Concepts**
Design Firm: **Modern Arts Packaging, New York, NY**
Distributor: **Modern Arts Packaging, New York, NY**

Among the newest concepts in package design is the gift bag, used in lieu of wrapping paper. At its most sophisticated, this type of bag incorporates coordinated tissue and/or ribbons. In these two prototype bags, Modern Arts Packaging has used both in two very different ways. The first bag features an illustration of a kite set against a white background, with vivid pink tissue. The fun is embodied in the kite's tail, which is three-dimensional. This tail will twist in the slightest breeze as it is carried down the street by a gift giver. The second bag employs a sophisticated foil finish and a complicated "X" figure ribbon construct. Both bags provide an interesting alternative to ordinary gift wrap.

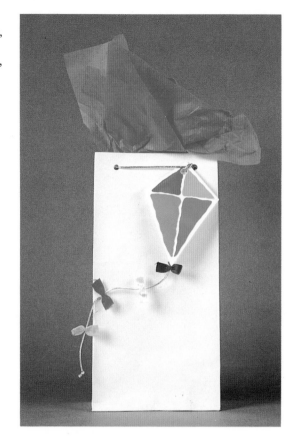

Shopping Bag Title: **Cherchez, Ltd.**
Establishment: **Cherchez, Ltd., New York, NY**
Designer: **Richard Giglio, New York**
Distributor: **Gaylord Specialties, New York, NY**
Materials
Paper: **Clay Coat**
Handle Type: **Twisted Paper**

"*Cherchez*" is the French word for "search." One might search for a long while before finding a comparably elegant store. Specializing in antique linens, pomanders, sachets and the like, Cherchez is a tiny outpost of civilization in a hurly-burly world. This inherent attitude is reflected in its packaging. Its shopping bags, with coordinated tissue and ribbon, are designed to be used as gift bags. The simple two-color pattern is reminiscent of 19th-century bandboxes. The overall effect of the consistent image is as modern as a space station.

Shopping Bag Title:	Lario
Establishment:	Lario, Hong Kong
Designer:	Alan Chan/Alvin Chan
Art Director:	Alan Chan
Firm:	Alan Chan Design Company, Wanchai, Hong Kong
Materials	
Paper:	Coated
Coating:	Laminate
Handle Type:	Plastic
Special Finishing:	Hand Finished

This leather boutique specializes in high-quality women's shoes and handbags imported from Europe. The surrealist bag design is an unusual rendering of a classic fantasy concerning shoes. Cinderella's glass slipper is depicted as an exceptionally high-heeled pump set against a red and black marble stair. The quality printing, laminate finish and hand-applied handles increase the fantasy's appeal.

Shopping Bag Title:	Eddie Lau
Establishment:	Eddie Lau, Hung Hom, Hong Kong
Designer:	Alvin Chan
Art Director:	Alan Chan/Alvin Chan
Firm:	Alan Chan Design Company, Wanchai, Hong Kong
Materials	
Paper:	Coated
Coating:	Laminate
Handle Type:	Soft Cord
Special Finishing:	Hand Finished

This well-known Hong Kong fashion designer is noted for his European-cut clothes with an Asian touch. To underscore this dual image, an Asian symbol with which westerners could readily identify—the pink "Pearl of the Orient"—was chosen as the main identity component for his retail store. The pearl is depicted floating against a stylized Asian landscape executed in black, white and a faint pink on a richly textured laminated paper. Black, soft cord handles complement the bag's elegance.

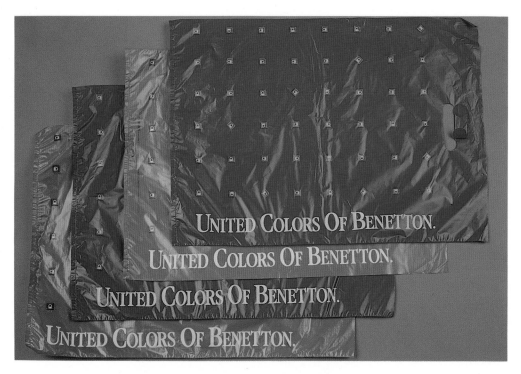

Shopping Bag Title:	Hi-Density Die-Cut
Establishment:	Benetton Services Corporation, New York, NY
Design Firm:	Eurobags International, Treviso, Italy
Manufacturer:	Eurobags International, Treviso, Italy
Distributor:	Eurobags U.S.A., Homewood, IL
Materials	
Bag:	High-Density Poly
Handle Type:	Die-Cut

By using a tiny version of the company logo as a repeat pattern, these bags maintain the consistency of Benetton's identity. By playing the pattern against a variety of different colored plastics, the bags maintain a fresh image. Note that the handles are die-cut from the body of the bag. Yet, to maintain the customer's comfort in handling, the portion of the bag which has been cut away for the handle is retained to be folded under to shield the bearer's hand from a cut plastic surface.

Shopping Bag Title:	Colors
Establishment:	Benetton Service Corporation, New York, NY
Design Firm:	Eurobags International, Treviso, Italy
Manufacturer:	Eurobags International, Treviso, Italy
Distributor:	Eurobags U.S.A., Homewood, IL
Manufacturer:	Eurobags International, Treviso, Italy
Materials	
Paper:	Coated
Coating:	Laminated
Handle Type:	Satin Cord

This bag is a compromise between an envelope and a miniature version of the traditional shopping bag, and was designed as a promotion for Benetton's signature cologne. The vivid colors used on the bag are intensified by the laminate coating. The hand-applied green satin ribbon pulls through the two envelope-style holes at the top of the Euro-style bag to both close it and form a dainty handle.

Shopping Bag Title:	**Gift Bag**
Establishment:	**Benetton Service Corporation, New York, NY**
Design Firm:	**Eurobags International, Treviso, Italy**
Manufacturer:	**Eurobags International, Treviso, Italy**
Distributor:	**Eurobags U.S.A., Homewood, IL**
Materials	
Bag:	**Mylar**
Handle Type:	**Self-Seal Closure**

This bag is almost the prototypical bag of the 80's. It employs an unusual material—mylar, and an unusual closure—it seals itself, rather like some sandwich bags. Above all, the imprinted image is slick and vivid. Designed and produced in Italy, these black mylar bags accept inks in a way paper and most plastic bags cannot. The overall effect is similar to oil-streaked puddles after a sudden rainstorm. It is easy to imagine the stir these can create on a busy street.

Shopping Bag Title: **Shop on Union Square**
Establishment: **Macy's California,**
San Francisco, CA
Designer: **Max Seabaugh**
Art Director: **Richard Nodine**
Firm: **Macy's Graphic Design,**
San Francisco, CA
Illustrator: **Max Seabaugh**

The Shop on Union Square carries
upper-end ready-to-wear clothing for
women. Though it can be reached
from the main department store, it has
its own entrance directly onto Union
Square, San Francisco's most elegant
shopping area. The crane logo was
developed based on antique furniture
in the shop. The cool silver, black and
white used for this bag are in marked
contrast to the vivid colors used in the
store's other bags. This is selling at its
softest.

Shopping Bag Title:	Vittorio Ricci
Establishment:	Vittorio Ricci, New York, NY
Designer:	Ine Wijtvliet
Firm:	Whitefleet Design Inc., New York, NY
Distributor:	Modern Arts Packaging, New York, NY
Materials	
Paper:	Coated
Coating:	Laminate
Special Finishing:	Printed Four-Color, White Dropout
Handle Type:	Soft Cord

This elegant, Euro-style shopping bag is a good example of the modern trend towards making the bag an architectural extension of the store. The stripe motif is drawn from fabrics used in the store's interior. Exterior signage and a variety of sales slips are also keyed to this identity program. The contrast between the classic stripes and the torn paper effect was intended to emphasize the fact that the store had branched out from strictly classic designer shoes to include contemporary designs in its stock as well.

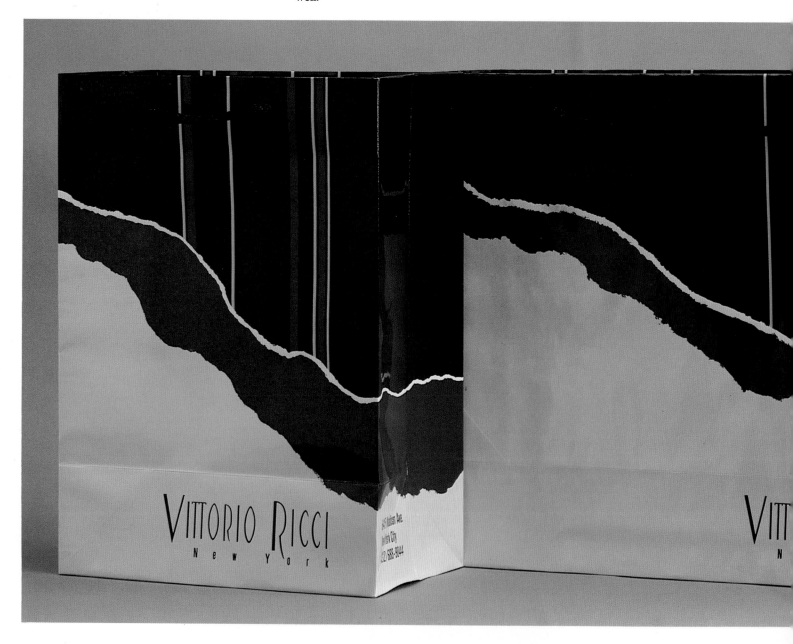

Shopping Bag Title:	**Steuben Glass**
Establishment:	**Steuben Glass, New York, NY**
Design Firm:	**Steuben Design Department**
Distributor:	**Weiss & Sons, Glendale, NY**
Materials	
	Hand-Assembled
Handle Type:	**Plastic**

If your product is exquisitely beautiful, why hide it in an opaque bag? If your product is fine crystal, all the more reason to display it for all to see. This is the reasoning behind Steuben's clear plastic bag. The opaque white top defines the bag's shape, provides a non-obtrusive place to attach the handles, and visually balances the white cardboard insert at the bottom.

Shopping Bag Title:	**Pace**
Establishment:	**Pace Boutique, Tsimshatsui, Hong Kong**
Designer:	**Alan Chan/Benjamin Lau**
Art Director:	**Alan Chan**
Firm:	**Alan Chan Design Company, Wanchai, Hong Kong**
Materials	
Paper:	**Coated**
Coating:	**Laminate**
Handle Type:	**Soft Cord**
Special Finishing:	**Hand Finished**

This bag is an architectural extension of the store. The granite-look background is based on the granite which is one of the major design components in the store. The Art Deco typeface on this Euro-style bag was designed to reflect the modern and slightly high-tech style of the interior design. Hand-finished, soft cord handles complete the bag. Note that the same design works for both the shopping bag and the dress pack.

Shopping Bag Title:	**Liz Claiborne**
Establishment:	**Liz Claiborne Inc.,**
	New York, NY
Designer:	**Bill Polito**
Art Director:	**Bill Polito/Shirley Shung**
Firm:	**Bill Polito Design**
	Consultant, New York, NY
Distributor:	**Modern Arts Packaging,**
	New York, NY
Materials	
Bag:	**Low Density Polypropelene**
Handle Type:	**Soft Cord**
Special Finishing:	**Matte and Glossy Inks**

This shopping bag was inspired by a hang tag devised by the designer. It features several unusual elements. Matte inks are played against a glossy ink background for textural interest. The shoulder strap permits the shopper to carry purchases while keeping both hands free. The use of vivid primary colors instills a note of fun. The shadow of the grid and card on the bag give the design depth. Coordinated pieces include the original hang tag, the stationery and a portfolio.

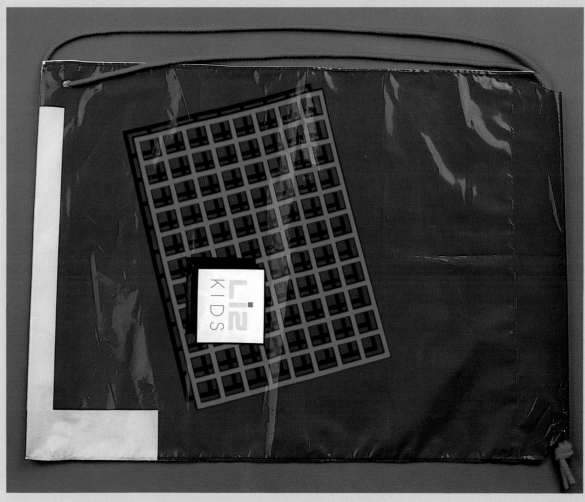

Shopping Bag Title:	**Playing Card**
	Promotional Bag
Establishment:	**Uniflex, New York, NY**
Designer:	**Warner J. Heuman**
Art Director:	**Al Heimlich**
Firm:	**Uniflex, Inc.,**
	New York, NY
Manufacturer:	**Uniflex, Inc., Westbury, NY**
Materials	
Bag:	**Polyethylene**
Handle Type:	**Molded Ridged Loop Style**
Special Finishing:	**Double wall constructed**

With the advent of plastic shopping bags, new printing techniques have been developed. Printing on plastic is subject to scuffing and transfer of the inks to the clothing of the bearer. This manufacturer solved the problem with double-wall construction. The inner wall provides an opaque background; the outer wall is clear plastic, with the printing executed on the *inside* surface. Neither the bearer's clothing, nor the items carried come into contact with the inks used—and the graphic image remains unsullied by the wear and tear of normal usage.

Glossary

Beam Bag™   A finishing technique whereby up to five inks and one coating are cured using an electron beam. Both matte and glossy finishes can be obtained with this process.

Coated Paper   Coated papers do not absorb ink. Instead, the inks float on the surface of the coating. To preserve the integrity of the reproduced image, coated paper bags must always be varnished.

Dot Gain   The process of impression on the substrate increases the size of an individual dot of color. To ensure that the dots are the desired size, adjustments can be made to the camera-ready art.

Grommet   A metal ring which reinforces the holes on certain hand-finished, soft cord-handled bags.

Gusset   On shopping bags, the narrow width of the bag where it is folded for shipping and storage.

Halftone   Creation of an image through the use of dots of various sizes.

Hand-Finishing   Usually refers to the turning under of the top of a bag to present a finished, rather than serrated, upper edge, or to the application of some handle types, especially soft cord. Both processes are accomplished by hand, rather than with machinery.

Handle Types Handles are made of extruded or molded plastic, twisted or flat paper, soft cord of either polyethelene or fabric, and sometimes flat cloth. Choice of one type over another is dictated by economics, bag design and projected end use.

Knock Out Reversal or removal of copy areas from a background color which will be overprinted in a second color.

Kraft Paper An uncoated stock available in either natural or white. White Kraft is achieved by the addition of bleach to the paper pulp. Absorbency and ease of imprinting vary with the starch content. At later stages of the production process, dyes can be introduced or varnishes applied.

Plastic Petroleum derivative used as an alternative to paper in the construction of shopping bags that accepts inks readily, but tends to stretch.

Roll-to-Roll Printing Process which permits printing of bags on an extremely wide web. Use of the second roll to transport the printed stock to converting equipment prevents distortion of the image due to stretching. Excellent registration is possible with this technique.

Screen Uniform measurement of dots per square inch. A 65-line screen (the most common size for flexographically printed shopping bags) contains 65 dots per square inch. The size of the dots determines the density of the ink coverage.

Trapping Overprinting two or more colors to prevent unprinted areas from showing due to small movements in printing registration.

Source: Champion International Corporation, Walden, NY

Selected Readings and References

Baker, Stephen, 1961. *Visual Persuasion.* New York, NY. McGraw-Hill Book Company, Inc.

Heller, Steven, and Guarnaccia, Steven, May 1985. *Big Bag Boom. PRINT:* 62-69.

Heller, Steven, and Chwast, Seymour, October 7, 1985. *From Sandwich Board to Objet d'Art. Adweek:* D45.

McKim, Robert H., 1980 *Thinking Visually: A Strategy Manual for Problem Solving*. Belmont, CA. *Lifetime Learning Publications*.

Oliver, Richard B., 1978. *Bandboxes and Shopping Bags*. Washington, D.C. *The Smithsonian Institution*.

Stich, Sandra, 1987. *Made in U.S.A.: An Americanization in Modern Art, the '50's & '60s*. Berkeley, CA. *University of California Press*.

Tanen Haus, Ruth Amdur, 1976. *Homage to the Bag. Museum of Contemporary Crafts of the American Arts Council*.

Various, April 9, 1987. *Summer of Love: 20 Years Later. San Francisco Chronicle*: 25-31.

Wagner, Stephen C., and Closen, Michael L., 1986. *The Shopping Bag: Portable Art*. New York, NY. *Crown Publishers*

Index

Firms

Manufacturer

Designers

Index

Clients